KT-578-845

Brand

When Ibsen wrote *Brand* in Italy in 1865 he had been writing plays for sixteen years – years of failure and poverty. It was not performed until 1885, but its publication in 1866 established his reputation in Scandinavia. The first production of *Brand* in England was in 1912, when it was given a single performance at the Royal Court Theatre. The next full-length London production was in 1959, when Michael Meyer's translation was performed at the Lyric Opera House, Hammersmith. For London audiences and critics this production was a revelation.

'Brand is a tremendous play . . . This is the most exciting theatrical experience to be found in London.'   Derek Monsey in the *Sunday Express*

'It is obvious, once one has seen the piece in Michael Meyer's extremely judicious abridgement and translation (rhythmical but unrhymed) that there are opportunities here equal to those in *Lear* . . . This production rather dwarfs everything else in the recent London Theatre.'

J. W. Lambert in *Drama*

The photograph on the front cover shows Patrick McGoohan and Olive McFarland in a scene from the 1959 production at the Lyric Opera House, Hammersmith. Photo: Ivor Sharp. The photograph of Ibsen on the back cover is reproduced by courtesy of the Mansell Collection.

Methuen's Theatre Classics

Henrik Ibsen

BRAND

Translated from the Norwegian by
MICHAEL MEYER

EYRE METHUEN LTD

LONDON

First published in Great Britain by
Rupert Hart-Davis Ltd 1960
© *Michael Meyer* 1960
First published in this paperback
edition by Methuen and Co Ltd 1967
Reprinted 1973 *by Eyre Methuen Ltd*
11 *New Fetter Lane*
London EC4P 4EE
SBN 413 30900 2
Printed Offset Litho in Great Britain by
Cox & Wyman Ltd, Fakenham, Norfolk

All rights whatsoever in this translation are strictly reserved, and applications for performance, etc., by professional and amateur companies in all countries except the United States of America and Canada should be made to:

Margaret Ramsay Ltd
14 Goodwin's Court
London WC2
England

In the United States and Canada, application should be made to:

International Famous Agency
1301 Avenue of the Americas
New York, New York 10019
U.S.A.

No performance may be given unless a licence has been obtained.

This book is sold subject to the condition that it shall not, by way of trade or otherwise, be lent, resold, hired out, or otherwise circulated without the publisher's prior consent in any form of binding or cover other than that in which it is published and without a similar condition including this condition being imposed on the subsequent purchaser.

Henrik Johan Ibsen

1828   Born at Skien in south-east Norway on 20 March, the second child of Knud Ibsen, a merchant, and his wife Marichen, *née* Altenburg.

1834–5 Father becomes ruined. The family moves to Venstoep, a few miles outside Skien.

1844   Ibsen (aged fifteen) becomes assistant to an apothecary at Grimstad, a tiny seaport further down the coast. Stays there for six years in great poverty.

1846   Has an illegitimate son with a servant-girl, Else Sofie Jensen.

1849   Writes his first play, CATILINE (in verse).

1850   Leaves Grimstad to become a student in Christiania (now Oslo). Writes second play, THE WARRIOR'S BARROW.

1851   Is invited to join Ole Bull's newly formed National Theatre at Bergen. Does so, and stays six years, writing, directing, designing costumes and keeping the accounts.

1852   Visits Copenhagen and Dresden to learn about the theatre. Writes ST JOHN'S EVE, a romantic comedy in verse and prose.

1853   ST JOHN'S EVE acted at Bergen. Failure.

1854   Writes LADY INGER OF OESTRAAT, an historical tragedy in prose.

1855   LADY INGER OF OESTRAAT acted at Bergen. Failure. Writes THE FEAST AT SOLHAUG, another romantic verse-and-prose comedy.

1856   THE FEAST AT SOLHAUG acted at Bergen. His first success. Meets Suzannah Thoresen. Writes OLAF LILJEKRANS, a third verse-and-prose comedy.

1857 OLAF LILJEKRANS acted at Bergen. Failure. Leaves Bergen to become artistic manager of the Christiania Norwegian Theatre. Writes THE VIKINGS AT HELGELAND, an historical prose tragedy

1858 Marries Suzannah Thoresen. THE VIKINGS AT HELGELAND staged. Small success.

1859 His only child, Sigurd, born.

1860–1 Years of poverty and despair. Unable to write.

1862 Writes LOVE'S COMEDY, a modern verse satire, his first play for five years. It is rejected by his own theatre, which goes bankrupt.

1863 Ibsen gets part-time job as literary adviser to the Danish-controlled Christiania Theatre. Extremely poor. Applies unsuccessfully to Government for financial support. Resorts to moneylenders. Writes THE PRETENDERS, another historical prose tragedy. Is granted a travel stipend by the Government; this is augmented by a collection raised by Bjoernson and other friends.

1864 THE PRETENDERS staged in Christiania. A success. He leaves Norway and settles in Rome. Remains resident abroad for the next twenty-seven years. Begins EMPEROR AND GALILEAN.

1865 Writes BRAND, in verse (as a play for reading, not acting), in Rome and Ariccia.

1866 BRAND published. Immense success; Ibsen becomes famous throughout Scandinavia (but it is not acted for nineteen years).

1867 Writes PEER GYNT, in verse (also to be read, not acted), in Rome, Ischia and Sorrento. It, too, is a great success; but is not staged for seven years.

1868 Moves from Rome and settles in Dresden.

1869   Attends opening of Suez Canal as Norwegian delegate. Completes THE LEAGUE OF YOUTH, a modern prose comedy.

1871   Revises his shorter poems and issues them in a volume. His farewell to verse; for the rest of his life he publishes exclusively in prose.

1873   Completes (after nine years) EMPEROR AND GALILEAN, his last historical play. Begins to be known in Germany and England.

1874   Returns briefly to Norway for first time in ten years. The students hold a torchlight procession in his honour.

1875   Leaves Dresden after seven years and settles in Munich. Begins THE PILLARS OF SOCIETY, the first of his twelve great modern prose dramas.

1876   PEER GYNT staged for first time. THE VIKINGS AT HELGELAND is performed in Munich, the first of his plays to be staged outside Scandinavia.

1877   Completes THE PILLARS OF SOCIETY. This makes him famous in Germany, where it is widely acted.

1878   Returns for one year to Italy.

1879   Writes A DOLL'S HOUSE in Rome and Amalfi. It causes an immediate sensation, and makes Ibsen internationally famous. Returns to Munich for a year.

1880   Resettles in Italy for a further five years. First performance of an Ibsen play in England (THE PILLARS OF SOCIETY for a single matinée in London).

1881   Writes GHOSTS in Rome and Sorrento. Violently attacked; all theatres reject it, and bookshops return it to the publisher.

1882   Writes AN ENEMY OF THE PEOPLE in Rome. Cordially received. GHOSTS receives its first performance (in Chicago), and is staged at last in Europe.

1884   Writes THE WILD DUCK in Rome and Gossensass. It,
        and all his subsequent plays, were regarded as obscure
        and were greeted with varying degrees of bewilder-
        ment.

1885   Revisits Norway again, for the first time since 1874.
        Leaves Rome and resettles in Munich.

1886   Writes ROSMERSHOLM in Munich.

1888   Writes THE LADY FROM THE SEA in Munich.

1889   Meets and becomes infatuated with the eighteen-year-
        old Emilie Bardach in Gossensass. Does not see her
        again, but the experience shadows the remainder of his
        writing. Janet Achurch acts Nora in London, the first
        major English-speaking production of Ibsen.

1890   Writes HEDDA GABLER in Munich.

1891   Returns to settle permanently in Norway.

1892   Writes THE MASTER BUILDER in Christiania.

1894   Writes LITTLE EYOLF in Christiania.

1896   Writes JOHN GABRIEL BORKMAN in Christiania.

1899   Writes WHEN WE DEAD AWAKEN in Christiania.

1901   First stroke. Partly paralysed.

1903   Second stroke. Left largely helpless.

1906   Dies in Christiania on 23 May, aged seventy-eight.

Introduction

In 1863 Ibsen's fortunes were at their lowest ebb. He had written nine plays, six of them historical. Of these the first, *Catiline*, had never been performed; *The Warrior's Barrow*, *St John's Eve*, *Lady Inger of Oestraat* and *Olaf Liljekrans* had appeared, all with disastrous results; only two, *The Feast at Solhaug* and *The Vikings at Helgeland*, had achieved any recognition at all, and that very limited. Worst of all, his most recent play, *Love's Comedy*, had been rejected, and the Norwegian Theatre of Christiania, where he had for seven years been artistic director, had gone bankrupt. Thus, at the age of thirty-five, he found himself virtually penniless, dependent on a tiny university grant and an even tinier salary which he received from the Danish Theatre of Christiania as literary adviser. With a wife and small son to support, he had to resort to moneylenders. Moreover, the Norwegian Parliament had rejected his application for a poet's stipend, while granting the applications of his fellow-poets Bjoernson and Vinje.

Fortunately, just when he must have been very close to despair, he achieved his first real success, with *The Pretenders*. First staged on 17 January 1864, it was presented eight times in less than two months – 'a success', says Professor Halvdan Koht, 'unique for a play as long and serious as this in a town as small as the Christiania of those days. . . . Now for the first time he rested in a full and free confidence in his own ability to write, and in his calling as a poet.'

At this juncture another piece of good fortune came his way, for he received the news that an order in council had allotted him 400 specie-dollars (about £100) for foreign travel. This was, in fact, much too small a sum to enable him to undertake the long journey southwards on which he had set his heart, but Bjoernson helped him to scrape together a little more, and when the ice broke in the spring of 1864 Ibsen set off towards Rome.

The war between Denmark and Germany over Schleswig-Holstein had just broken out, and the refusal of Norway and Sweden to help her Scandinavian neighbour angered Ibsen. While he was in Copenhagen that April, on the way to Rome, news arrived of the fall of Dybboel to German troops; and next month, when he reached Berlin, he saw the Danish cannons captured at Dybboel being led in triumph through the streets of the capital, while Germans lining the route spat at them. 'It was for me', Ibsen wrote, 'a sign that, some day, history would spit in the eyes of Sweden and Norway for their part in this affair.' Later, looking back on this period, he wrote: 'It was now that *Brand* began to grow inside me like a foetus.'

He reached Rome in the middle of June. A few days later the Scandinavian community there held a small farewell party before breaking up to go to the country and so escape the summer heat. Ibsen attended this party, and his friend Lorenz Dietrichson has described the scene. 'It was the first evening for some while that Ibsen had spent among Scandinavians, and he began to speak of the painful and disturbing impressions of recent events in the war which he had received on his journey. Gradually and almost imperceptibly, his talk took on the character of an improvised speech; all the bitterness which had for so long been stored up within him, all the fiery indignation and passion for the Scandinavian cause which he had bottled up for so long, found an outlet. His voice began to ring, and in the evening dusk one saw only his burning eyes. When he had finished, no one cried Bravo or raised his glass, but I think we all felt that that evening the Marseillaise of the North had rung out into the Roman night air.'

Writing to his mother-in-law, Magdalene Thoresen, Ibsen angrily described how Danes in Rome were attending Sunday service in the German church, and sat silent in their pews while the German pastor prayed for victory for the Prussian arms in their righteous cause.

After a fortnight in Rome, Ibsen moved out to the small hill town of Genzano, and stayed there for two months. Lorenz Dietrichson was living there with his family, and it was during a conversation with Dietrichson that Ibsen first conceived the idea of writing a tragedy about the Emperor Julian – the play that, slowly and with many interruptions, developed over the next nine years into *Emperor and Galilean*. It was in Genzano, too, that he began to write an epic poem. Shortly after he returned to Rome in the autumn, he mentioned in a letter that 'for some time I have been working on a big poem', optimistically adding that he hoped to have both that and the play about Julian ready by the following spring or summer. This poem was called *Brand*.

Ibsen based it on a Danish poem written some twenty years previously, Frederik Paludan-Müller's *Adam Homo*. Paludan-Müller's chief character was an everyday man who shunned ideals and compromised incessantly with the world and with himself. Ibsen intended his chief character to be the exact opposite of *Adam Homo* – a man who shunned compromise.

Then, in September, a young Norwegian named Christopher Bruun arrived in Rome.

He was a theologian, but was hesitating to take Holy Orders because he felt that life and the teaching of the Norwegian State Church were incompatible. Like Ibsen, he had been angered by the German attack on Denmark but, unlike Ibsen, he had volunteered as a soldier, and had fought with the Danes at the battle of Dybboel. Ibsen got to know Bruun at once – he had already seen a good deal of Bruun's mother and sister at Genzano. They discussed the war, and Bruun asked Ibsen why, if he felt so strongly, he had not volunteered himself. 'We poets have other tasks to perform,' Ibsen replied; but a doubt remained in his mind. He wondered whether he had been right to compromise; and with this doubt was linked another. Was he right to believe so inflexibly in his calling as a writer and thus, in all probability, condemn his wife and child to continued poverty so that he might follow this calling?

Ibsen had already decided to make the chief character of his long poem a discontented priest, and had at first based him on his own memories of a revivalist named G. A. Lammers, who had converted Ibsen's parents and brothers in Skien during the eighteen-fifties. Bruun's personality now began to intrude into the character of Brand, and his ideas into the subject-matter of the poem. Ibsen struggled painfully with it throughout the autumn, winter, spring and summer, while at the same time doing historical research for *Emperor and Galilean*. At length, in July 1865, at Ariccia, a small town south of Rome, he threw aside the poem, of which he had completed some two hundred stanzas, and decided to rewrite it as a poetic drama.

At first this, too, progressed slowly and with difficulty. Ibsen has described how the turning-point came. In a letter to Bjoernson, dated 12 September 1865, he wrote:

'I did not know where to turn. Then, one day, I went into St Peter's – I had gone into Rome on some business – and suddenly everything I wanted to say appeared to me in a strong and clear light. I had thrown overboard the work with which I had been torturing myself for a year without getting anywhere, and in the middle of July I started on something new which has been making such progress as no other work of mine has ever done. . . . It is a dramatic poem, of serious content; contemporary subject-matter – five acts in rhymed verse (but no *Love's Comedy*). The fourth act is almost finished, and I feel I shall be able to complete the fifth in a week. I work both morning and afternoon, which I have never been able to do before. It is blessedly peaceful out here; no one I know. I read nothing but the Bible.'

Ibsen finished the dramatic version of *Brand* in three months. The fifth act (about a third of the play) took longer than the week he had predicted, but he managed it in a little under five weeks, and by mid-October the play was ready to be posted to his Danish publisher, Hegel of Gyldendal's. Hegel could not get it out in time for Christmas, as Ibsen had hoped, and it was not until 15 March 1866 that *Brand* appeared on the bookstalls. It created an immediate and widespread sensation throughout Scandinavia, where the movement toward liberalism and individualism was just reaching its climax. *Brand* stated sharply and vividly the necessity of following one's private conscience and 'being oneself' and it ran quickly through three editions. A fourth was in the press by the end of the year. Georg Brandes has described the effect which *Brand* had on the Scandinavia of the time:

'It was a book which left no reader cold. Every receptive and unblunted mind felt, on closing the book, a penetrating, nay, an overwhelming impression of having stood face to face with a great and indignant genius, before whose piercing glance weakness felt itself compelled to cast down its eyes. What made the impression less definite, namely, the fact that this mastermind was not quite clear and transparent, rendered it, on the other hand, all the more fascinating.'

And August Strindberg, who was seventeen when *Brand* appeared, later called it 'the voice of a Savonarola'.

The influence of Paludan-Müller's *Adam Homo* on *Brand* has already been noted. Another important literary influence may (though some dispute it) have been the Danish philosopher Kierkegaard. Georg Brandes, writing the year after *Brand* appeared, observed: 'It actually seems as if Ibsen had aspired to the honour of being called Kierkegaard's poet'; and it has been suggested that it was Kierkegaard's *Either-Or* which gave Ibsen the idea of 'All or Nothing'. A more probable influence, in my opinion, is Kierkegaard's *Fear and Trembling*, which dwells continually on the legend of Abraham and Isaac. 'No one was as great as Abraham, and who is capable of under-

standing him ?' the sentence might well serve to sum up *Brand*.
There are other sentences in *Fear and Trembling* which apply
to *Brand*: 'There was the man who was great through his
strength, and the man who was great through his wisdom, and
the man who was great through his hope, and the man who was
great through his love; but Abraham was greater than any of
these, great through the power whose strength is weakness,
great through the wisdom whose secret is foolishness, great
through the hope whose expression is madness, great through
the love which is hatred of oneself.' And elsewhere there is a
reference to 'that vast passion which disdains the fury of the
elements and the powers of creation in order to battle with
God'. Moreover *Fear and Trembling* contains a long section
on the legend of Agnes and the Triton, and I think it possible
that Ibsen, consciously or unconsciously, may have taken his
heroine's name from this passage. He based the character of
Agnes largely on Bruun's sister, Thea; and Bruun was an
ardent disciple of Kierkegaard.

A journey which Ibsen had made through the Norwegian
countryside in 1862 to gather folk-lore also left its mark on
the play. Many of the descriptions of natural scenery in *Brand*
stem from this journey – for example, the steep descent from
the Sogn mountains, and the dangers of life in a fjordside
village with its storms and landslips.

Although the character of Brand was based partly on that
of the revivalist, G. A. Lammers, and partly on that of
Christopher Bruun, Ibsen also, by his own admission, put a
good deal of himself into the part: 'Brand,' he once said, 'is
myself in my best moments.' He later wrote to Georg Brandes
that he could, in fact, as easily have made Brand a sculptor or
a politician, or even Galileo – 'except that then of course he
would have to have held strongly to his beliefs, and not pre-
tended that the earth stood still'. I suspect that Ejnar, the painter,
represented Ibsen's idea of himself in his worst moments; Ibsen
was an accomplished painter and in his youth had seriously

considered following art instead of literature as a profession.

A great deal has been written about the symbolism of *Brand*, and the different significances that might be attached to the hawk, the Ice Church, and so forth. Dr Arne Duve, in his stimulating book *Symbolikken i Henrik Ibsens Skuespill*, suggests that the hawk represents the life of the emotions, i.e. love, and that it is Brand's fear of the powers of life and light that makes him, in the fifth act, dismiss the hawk contemptuously as 'the spirit of compromise'. The Ice Church, Dr Duve thinks, represents the opposite of the hawk, i.e. the negation of love. Gerd, like Brand, fears and distrusts love (like him, she is the daughter of a loveless marriage), and Brand's negation of love finally leads him, too, to the terrible citadel of the Ice Church; what Ibsen, thirty years later in *John Gabriel Borkman*, was to term 'the coldness of the heart'. The Ice Church finally killed Brand, just as the coldness of the heart killed John Gabriel Borkman. On the other hand, Mr Michael Elliott, who directed the 1959 production of *Brand* at the Lyric Opera House, Hammersmith, thinks that the hawk represents nothing as specific as love, but rather in a general way, 'whatever one rejects', just as Room 101 in George Orwell's *1984* contained 'the worst thing in the world', whatever that might be. I agree with this theory, and believe that the Ice Church stands for the false citadel which each of us builds in his own imagination as a refuge from his particular hawk.

Ibsen never intended *Brand* for the stage; he wrote it, as he wrote *Peer Gynt* eighteen months later, simply to be read. His years as a dramatist and a theatre director had made him bitterly aware of the technical limitations of the theatre and its audiences. Consequently he chose a form in which he need make no concessions to these limitations. He wrote scenes which demand, among other things, a storm at sea and an avalanche; and his final version was, like *Peer Gynt*, more than twice the length of an average play.

Despite *Brand*'s success with the reading public, nineteen years passed before anyone attempted to stage it. At length, on 24 March 1885, Ludvig Josephson presented it at Nya Teatern in Stockholm. August Lindberg has described the first night. 'It lasted for six and a half hours, until 12.30 a.m. Such ladies as survived to the end lay dozing on their escorts' shoulders, with their corsets and bodices unbuttoned.' In spite of its length, however, the play proved a success, and during the next two decades *Brand* was performed in almost every European country which boasted a serious theatre, except England. Lugné-Poe produced it at his Théâtre de L'Oeuvre in Paris in 1895, and it was staged in several towns in Germany around the turn of the century. Strangely enough, it was not produced in Norway until 1904, but it has since been revived there on a number of occasions, and remains one of Ibsen's most admired and most quoted plays in his own country. It was especially successful in Russia in the early years of this century; it was introduced into the repertory of the Moscow Arts Theatre in 1907, and caused excitement by its outspoken criticisms of society. The Russians introduced it to America when they visited New York in 1912; and in 1928 the Pitoëffs scored a success with it in Paris, in a production which used ultra-simple décor.

England, as usual, had to wait longer than most other countries before seeing the play, although Edmund Gosse had written about it at considerable length as early as January 1873 (in a long article in the *Fortnightly Review* entitled 'Ibsen, the Norwegian Satirist'), and at least three separate translations into English had been made before the end of the century. In June 1893 the fourth act was presented as a curtain-raiser to *The Master Builder* for two matinées and two evening performances, during a three-weeks Ibsen season at the Opera Comique in London; Bernard Gould[1] played Brand, Elizabeth

[1] Alias Bernard Partridge, the well-known artist.

Robins Agnes, and Frances Ivor the Gipsy Woman. On 29
November 1911 the Ibsen Club staged the fourth act (with
the last act of *A Doll's House*) at the Ibsen Rehearsal Studio
in London, but the play was not presented in a complete form
until 10 November 1912, when the Irish actor, W. G. Fay,
produced it in William Wilson's prose translation at the Royal
Court Theatre for a single performance under the auspices
of the Play Actors. *The Times*, after deploring the omission of
the scene between Brand and his mother, and that in which
Brand decides to give up his first mission and settle down in the
fjordside village, went on:

'Mr W. G. Fay, the producer, had done his work well. . . .
The difficulties of arrangement he had overcome skilfully and
fairly. Into his company he had instilled some at least of the
speed which the passionate, soaring, plunging poem demands.
In the part of Agnes . . . Miss Phyllis Relph did well, especially in that wonderful scene where Agnes, having learned from
Brand to make the last sacrifice by giving away all her dead
baby's clothes to the gipsy woman, soars clean above Brand's
head and points him the way to his own goal. Miss Mignon
Clifford gave a very lively and understanding portrait of Gerd,
the wild girl. . . . As to the Brand of Mr H. A. Saintsbury,
we are in a difficulty. In appearance and bearing, he was so
wholly unlike our idea of Brand that we have not yet found
our way about his performance. It seemed, we must admit, very
experienced, very clever, and nothing more. But we can quite
believe that what we saw as a mincing, prelatical Brand, entirely
lacking the burliness, the vitality, the passion of the man, had
good qualities, which would emerge on further acquaintance.'

On 11 December 1936, Hilton Edwards produced *Brand* at
the Gate Theatre, Dublin, with Michael Mac Liammoir as
Brand and Meriel Moore as Agnes. The Cambridge A.D.C.
presented it at Cambridge in December 1945, in a production
by John Prudhoe, with Richard Bebb-Williams as Brand, Ann
Mankowitz as Agnes, and Lyndon Brook as Ejnar. A version

by James Forsyth was broadcast in the B.B.C. Third Programme on 11 December 1949, with Ralph Richardson as Brand, Sybil Thorndike as Brand's mother, Margaret Leighton as Agnes, and Louise Hutton as Gerd, and again on 30 December 1956, this time with Stephen Murray as Brand, Fay Compton as Brand's mother, Ursula Howells as Agnes and June Tobin as Gerd. Both productions were by Val Gielgud. Apart from the solitary performance in 1912, however, London had to wait until 8 April 1959 to see a full production of *Brand*. On that date it was presented at the Lyric Opera House, Hammersmith, by the 59 Theatre Company, in a production by Michael Elliott, with the cast named on page 19.

In 1906, when Ibsen was dying, Christopher Bruun, the man who had largely inspired the character of Brand nearly half a century before, came to visit him. The two had remained friends, and Bruun had baptized Ibsen's grandchild. They had always kept off the subject of religion, but now, in the presence of death, Bruun tentatively touched on the subject of Ibsen's relationship to God. Ibsen's answer was short and characteristic. 'You leave that to me!' he growled; and Bruun did.

MICHAEL MEYER

This translation was commissioned by the 59 Theatre Company, and presented by them on 8 April 1959, at the Lyric Opera House, Hammersmith. The cast was:

BRAND	Patrick McGoohan
A GUIDE	Robert Bernal
GUIDE'S SON	William McLaughlin
AGNES	Dilys Hamlett
EJNAR	Harold Lang
GERD	Olive McFarland
MAYOR	Patrick Wymark
WOMAN FROM THE HEADLAND	June Bailey
A VILLAGER	Fulton MacKay
SECOND VILLAGER	Frank Windsor
BRAND'S MOTHER	Enid Lorimer
DOCTOR	Peter Sallis
GIPSY WOMAN	Anita Giorgi
SEXTON	Robert Bernal
SCHOOLMASTER	Frank Windsor
PROVOST	Peter Sallis

Produced by Michael Elliott. Designed by Richard Negri.

The action takes place in and around a village on the west coast of Norway, and in the mountains above it.

Time: the middle of the last century.

ACT I High in the mountains
ACT II Scene I A village by the fjord
Scene II A farm above the fjord
ACT III Outside Brand's house
ACT IV Inside Brand's house
ACT V Scene I The new church
Scene II By the highest farm above the village
Scene III High in the mountains

Act One

In the snow, high up in the wilds of the mountains. Mist hangs densely. It is raining, and nearly dark. BRAND, *dressed in black, with pack and staff, is struggling towards the west. His companions, a* GUIDE *and the* GUIDE'S YOUNG SON, *follow a short distance behind.*

GUIDE (*shouts after* BRAND).
    Hi, there, stranger! Don't go so fast!
    Where are you?
BRAND. Here.
GUIDE. You'll lose your way. This mist's so thick
    I can hardly see the length of my staff.
SON. Father, there's a crack in the snow!
GUIDE. A crevasse!
BRAND. We have lost all trace of the path.
GUIDE (*shouts*). Stop, man, for God's sake. The glacier's
    As thin as a crust here. Tread lightly.
BRAND (*listening*). I can hear the roar of a waterfall.
GUIDE. A river has hollowed its way beneath us.
    There's an abyss here too deep to fathom.
    It will swallow us up.
BRAND. I must go on. I told you before.
GUIDE. It's beyond mortal power. Feel!
    The ground here is hollow and brittle.
    Stop! It's life or death.
BRAND. I must. I serve a great master.
GUIDE. What's his name?
BRAND. His name is God.
GUIDE. Who are you?
BRAND. A priest.

GUIDE (*goes cautiously closer*).
> Listen, priest. We've only one life.
> Once that's lost, we don't get another.
> There's a frozen mountain lake ahead,
> And mountain lakes are treacherous.

BRAND. We will walk across it.

GUIDE. Walk on water? (*Laughs.*)

BRAND. It has been done.

GUIDE. Ah, that was long ago. There are no miracles now.
> You sink without trace.

BRAND. Farewell. (*Begins to move on.*)

GUIDE. You'll die.

BRAND. If my master needs my death
> Then welcome flood and cataract and storm.

GUIDE (*quietly*). He's mad.

SON (*almost crying*).
> Father, let's turn back. There's a storm coming on.

BRAND (*stops, and goes back towards them*). Listen, guide.
> Didn't you say your daughter has sent you word
> That she is dying, and cannot go in peace
> Unless she sees you first?

GUIDE. It's true, God help me.

BRAND. And she cannot live beyond today?

GUIDE. Yes.

BRAND. Then, come!

GUIDE. It's impossible. Turn back.

BRAND (*gazes at him*).
> What would you give for your daughter to die in peace?

GUIDE. I'd give everything I have, my house and farm, gladly.

BRAND. But not your life?

GUIDE. My life?

BRAND. Well?

GUIDE. There's a limit. I've a wife and children at home.

BRAND. Go home. Your life is the way of death.
> You do not know God, and God does not know you.

GUIDE. You're hard.

SON (*tugging at his coat*). Come on, father.

GUIDE. All right. But he must come too.

BRAND. Must I ? (*Turns. A hollow roar is heard in the distance.*)

SON (*screams*). An avalanche!

BRAND (*to the* GUIDE, *who has grabbed him by the collar*). Let go!

GUIDE. No.

BRAND. Let go at once!

GUIDE (*wrestling with* BRAND). No, the Devil take me – !

BRAND (*tears himself loose, and throws the* GUIDE *in the snow*).
    He will, you can be sure. In the end.

GUIDE (*sits rubbing his arm*).
    Ah! Stubborn fool! But he's strong.
    So that's what he calls the Lord's work.
    (*Shouts, as he gets up.*) Hi, priest!

SON. He's gone over the pass.

GUIDE. I can still see him. (*Shouts again.*) Hi, there!
    Where did we leave the road ?

BRAND (*from the mist*).
    You need no signpost. Your road is broad enough.

GUIDE. I wish to God it was.
    Then I'd be warm at home by nightfall.

He and his SON *exeunt towards the east.*

BRAND (*appears higher up, and looks in the direction in which
        they have gone*).
    They grope their way home. You coward!
    If you'd had the will and only lacked the strength,
    I would have helped you. Footsore as I am,
    I could have carried you on my tired back
    Gladly and easily. (*Moves on again.*)
    Ha; how men love life! They'll sacrifice
    Anything else, but life – no, that must be saved.

He smiles, as though remembering something.

    When I was a boy, I remember,

Two thoughts kept occurring to me, and made me laugh.
An owl frightened by darkness, and a fish
Afraid of water. Why did I think of them?
Because I felt, dimly, the difference
Between what is and what should be; between
Having to endure, and finding one's burden
Unendurable.
     Every man
Is such an owl and such a fish, created
To work in darkness, to live in the deep;
And yet he is afraid. He splashes
In anguish towards the shore, stares at the bright
Vault of heaven, and screams: 'Give me air
And the blaze of day.'
What was that? It sounded like singing.
Yes, there it is – laughter and song.
The sun shines. The mist is lifting.
Now I see the whole mountain plain.
A happy crowd of people stands
In the morning sunshine on the mountain top.
Now they are separating. The others
Turn to the east, but two go westwards.
They wave farewell.

The sun breaks more brightly through the mist. He stands looking down at the approaching figures.

     Light shines about these two.
It is as though the mist fell back before them,
As though heather clothed every slope and ridge,
And the sky smiled on them. They must be
Brother and sister. Hand in hand they run
Over the carpet of heather.

EJNAR *and* AGNES, *warm and glowing, in light travelling clothes, come dancing along the edge of the crevasse. The mist has dispersed, and a clear summer morning lies over the mountain.*

EJNAR (*sings*). Agnes, my butterfly,
>   You know I will capture you yet.
>   Though you fly, it will not save you,
>   For soon you'll be caught in my net.
AGNES (*sings, dancing backwards in front of him, evading him
>   continuously*). If I am your butterfly,
>   With joy and delight I shall play,
>   But if you should catch me,
>   Don't crush my wings, I pray.
EJNAR. On my hand I shall lift you,
>   In my heart I shall lock you away,
>   And for ever, my butterfly,
>   Your joyful game you can play.

Without noticing it, EJNAR *and* AGNES *have come to the edge of
the crevasse, and now stand on the brink.*

BRAND (*calling down to them*).
>   Stop! You're on the edge of a precipice!
EJNAR. Who's that shouting?
AGNES (*points upwards*). Look!
BRAND. That snowdrift's hollow.
>   It's hanging over the edge of the precipice.
>   Save yourselves before it's too late!
EJNAR (*throws his arms round her and laughs up at him*).
>   We're not afraid.
AGNES.   We haven't finished
>   Our game; we've a whole lifetime yet.
EJNAR. We've been given a hundred years
>   Together in the sun.
BRAND.   And then?
EJNAR. Then? Home again. (*Points to the sky.*) To Heaven.
BRAND. Ah! That's where you've come from, is it?
EJNAR. Of course. Where else? Come down here,
>   And I'll tell you how good God has been to us.
>   Then you'll understand the power of joy.

Don't stand up there like an icicle. Come on down!
Good! First, I'm a painter,
And it's a wonderful thing to give my thoughts flight,
Charming dead colours into life
As God creates a butterfly out of a chrysalis.
But the most wonderful thing God ever did
Was to give me Agnes for my bride.
I was coming from the south, after a long
Journey, with my easel on my back –

AGNES (*eagerly*). As bold as a king, fresh and gay,
Knowing a thousand songs.

EJNAR. As I was coming through the pass, I saw her.
She had come to drink the mountain air,
The sunshine, the dew, and the scent of the pines.
Some force had driven me up to the mountains.
A voice inside me said:
'Seek beauty where the pine trees grow,
By the forest river, high among the clouds.'
There I painted my masterpiece,
A blush on her cheek, two eyes bright with happiness,
A smile that sang from her heart.
I asked her to marry me, and she said yes.
They gave a feast for us which lasted three days.
Everyone was there. We tried to slip away
Last night, but they followed us, waving flags,
Leaves in their hats, singing all the way.
The mist was heavy from the north,
But it fell back before us.

BRAND. Where are you going now?

EJNAR. Over that last mountain peak, westwards down
To the mouth of the fjord, and then home to the city
For our wedding feast as fast as ship can sail.
Then south together, like swans on their first flight –

BRAND. And there?

EJNAR.   A happy life

Together, like a dream, like a fairy tale.
For this Sunday morning, out there on the mountain,
Without a priest, our lives were declared free
Of sorrow, and consecrated to happiness.

BRAND. By whom?

EJNAR. By everyone.

BRAND. Farewell. (*Turns to go.*)

EJNAR (*suddenly looks closely at him in surprise*).
No, wait. Don't I know your face?

BRAND (*coldly*). I am a stranger.

EJNAR. I'm sure I remember –
Could we have known each other at school – or at
home?

BRAND. Yes, we were friends at school. But then
I was a boy. Now I am a man.

EJNAR. It can't be – (*Shouts suddenly.*) Brand! Yes, it's you!

BRAND. I knew you at once.

EJNAR. How good to see you!
Look at me! Yes, you're the same old Brand,
Who always kept to yourself and never played
With us.

BRAND. No, I was not at home
Among you southerners. I was
Of another race, born by a cold fjord,
In the shadow of a barren mountain.

EJNAR. Is your home in these parts?

BRAND. My road will take me through it.

EJNAR. Through it? You're going beyond, then?

BRAND. Yes, beyond; far beyond my home.

EJNAR. Are you a priest now?

BRAND. A mission preacher. I live
One day in one place, the next in another.

EJNAR. Where are you bound?

BRAND (*sharply*). Don't ask that.

EJNAR. Why?

BRAND (*changes his tone*).

    Well, the ship which is waiting for you will take me too.

EJNAR. Agnes, he's coming the same way!

BRAND. Yes; but I am going to a burial feast.

AGNES. To a burial feast?

EJNAR. Who is to be buried?

BRAND. That God you have just called yours.

AGNES. Come, Ejnar.

EJNAR. Brand!

BRAND. The God of every dull and earthbound slave
    Shall be shrouded and coffined for all to see
    And lowered into his grave. It is time, you know.
    He has been ailing for a thousand years.

EJNAR. Brand, you're ill!

BRAND.   No, I am well and strong
    As mountain pine or juniper. It is
    Our time, our generation, that is sick
    And must be cured. All you want is to flirt,
    And play, and laugh; to do lip-service to your faith
    But not to know the truth; to leave your suffering
    To someone who they say died for your sake.
    He died for you, so you are free to dance.
    To dance, yes; but whither?
    Ah, that is another thing, my friend.

EJNAR. Oh, I see. This is the new teaching.
    You're one of those pulpit-thumpers who tell us
    That all joy is vanity, and hope
    The fear of hell will drive us into sackcloth.

BRAND. No. I do not speak for the Church. I hardly
    Know if I'm a Christian. But I know
    That I am a man. And I know what it is
    That has drained away our spirit.

EJNAR (*smiles*). We usually have the reputation of being
    Too full of spirit.

BRAND.   You don't understand me.

It isn't love of pleasure that is destroying us.
It would be better if it were.
Enjoy life if you will,
But be consistent, do it all the time,
Not one thing one day and another the next.
Be wholly what you are, not half and half.
Everyone now is a little of everything;
A little solemn on Sundays, a little respectful
Towards tradition; makes love to his wife after Saturday
Supper, because his father did the same.
A little gay at feasts, a little lavish
In giving promises, but niggardly
In fulfilling them; a little of everything;
A little sin, a little virtue;
A little good, a little evil; the one
Destroys the other, and every man is nothing.

EJNAR. All right. I agree that we are sinful.
But what has that to do with Him
You want to bury – the God I still call mine?

BRAND. My gay friend, show me this God of yours.
You're an artist. You've painted him, I hear.
He's old, isn't he?

EJNAR.   Well – yes.

BRAND.   Of course.
And grey, and thin on top, as old men are?
Kindly, but severe enough to frighten
Children into bed? Did you give him slippers?
I hope you allowed him spectacles and a skull-cap.

EJNAR (*angrily*). What do you mean?

BRAND.   That's just what he is,
The God of our country, the people's God.
A feeble dotard in his second childhood.
You would reduce God's kingdom,
A kingdom which should stretch from pole to pole.
To the confines of the Church. You separate

Life from faith and doctrine. You do not want
To live your faith. For that you need a God
Who'll keep one eye shut. That God is getting feeble
Like the generation that worships him.
Mine is a storm where yours is a gentle wind,
Inflexible where yours is deaf, all-loving,
Not all-doting. And He is young
And strong like Hercules. His is the voice
That spoke in thunder when He stood
Bright before Moses in the burning bush,
A giant before the dwarf of dwarfs. In the valley
Of Gideon He stayed the sun, and worked
Miracles without number – and would work
Them still, if people were not dead, like you.

EJNAR (*smiles uncertainly*). And now we are to be created anew?

BRAND. Yes. As surely as I know that I
Was born into this world to heal its sickness
And its weakness.

EJNAR. Do not blow out the match because it smokes
Before the lantern lights the road.
Do not destroy the old language
Until you have created the new.

BRAND. I do not seek
To create anything new. I uphold
What is eternal. I do not come
To bolster dogmas or the Church.
They were born and they will die.
But one thing cannot die; the Spirit, not created, but
    eternal,
Redeemed by Christ when it had been forfeited
In the first fresh spring of time. He threw a bridge
Of human faith from flesh back to the Spirit's source.
Now it is hawked round piecemeal, but from these
    stumps
Of soul, from these severed heads and hands,

A whole shall rise which God shall recognize,
Man, His greatest creation, His chosen heir,
Adam, young and strong.

EJNAR (*interrupts*). Goodbye. I think we had better part.

BRAND. Go westwards. I go to the north. There are two
Roads to the fjord. One is as short as the other.
Farewell.

EJNAR. Goodbye.

BRAND (*turns as he is about to descend*).
There is darkness and there is light. Remember,
Living is an art.

EJNAR (*waving him away*). Turn the world upside down.
I still have faith in my God.

BRAND.   Good; but paint him
With crutches. I go to lay him in his grave.

He goes down the path. EJNAR *goes silently and looks after him.*

AGNES (*stands for a moment as though abstracted; then starts and
looks round uneasily*). Has the sun gone down?

EJNAR. No, it was only
A cloud passing. Soon it will shine again.

AGNES. There's a cold wind.

EJNAR.   It was a gust
Blowing through the gap. Let's go down.

AGNES. How black the mountain has become, shutting
Our road to the south.

EJNAR.   You were so busy singing
And playing, you didn't notice it until
He frightened you with his shouting. Let him follow
His narrow path. We can go on with our game.

AGNES. No, not now. I am tired.

EJNAR.   Yes, so am I;
And the way down isn't as easy
As the way we've come. Look, Agnes! You see
That blue streak over there with the sun on it?

That is the sea. And the dark smoke drifting along
The fjord, and that black speck which has just appeared
Off the headland? That is the steamer; yours,
And mine. Now it is moving into the fjord.
Tonight it will steam out into the open sea,
With you and me on board. Now the mist veils it,
Heavy and grey. Look, Agnes! Did you see
How the sea and sky seemed to paint each other?
AGNES (*gazes abstractedly*). Yes. But – did you see – ?
EJNAR. What?
AGNES (*speaks softly, as though in church*).
    How, as he spoke, he grew?

She goes down the path. EJNAR *follows.*

*The scene changes to a path along the mountain wall, with a wild
abyss beyond, to the right. Higher up, behind the mountain, can
be glimpsed higher peaks, covered with snow.* BRAND *comes along
the path, descends, stops half-way on a projecting rock, and looks
down into the abyss.*

BRAND. Yes. Now I know where I am. Every boathouse,
    Every cottage; the landslide hill,
    The birchtrees on the fjord, the old brown church,
    The elder bushes along the river bank.
    I remember it all
    From childhood. But it looks greyer now,
    And smaller. The snowdrift on the mountain
    Hangs further out than it used to. It cuts
    Even more from the valley's meagre strip of sky;
    It lowers, threatens, shadows, steals more sun.

He sits down and gazes into the distance.

    The fjord; was it as grim and narrow as this?
    A storm is blowing up. There's a ship
    Running for shelter. And there to the south

Under the shadow of a crag, I can see
A boat-house and a jetty, and behind them
A red cottage. The widow's cottage!
My childhood home!
          Memories swarm upon me,
And memories of memories. There, among
The stones on the shore, I lived my childhood alone.

A heavy weight lies on me, the burden
Of being tied to another human being
Whose spirit pointed earthwards. Everything
That I desired so passionately before
Trembles and fades. My strength and courage fail me,
My mind and soul are numbed.
Now, as I approach my home, I find
Myself a stranger; I awake bound, shorn,
And tamed, like Samson in the harlot's lap.

He looks down again into the valley.

What is all that activity?
From every cottage pour men, women and children.
Long lines of people wind up the narrow streets,
Towards the old church. (*Stands up.*)
          Oh, I know you through and through,
Dull souls and slovenly minds. Your prayers
Have not the strength nor the agony to reach
To Heaven – except to cry:
'Give us this day our daily bread!' That
Is now the watchword of this country, the remnant
Of its faith. Away from this stifling pit;
The air down here is poisoned, as in a mine.
Here no breeze can ever stir.

He is about to go when a stone thrown from above rolls down the path close to him.

BRAND (*shouts up*). Hallo, there! Who is throwing stones?

GERD, *a fifteen-year-old girl, runs along the mountain crest with stones in her apron.*

GERD. He screeched! I hit him!
  No, there he sits unhurt, rocking
  On that fallen branch.

She throws a stone again, and screams.

     Here he comes again,
  As savage as before. Help! Ah!
  He's tearing me with his claws!
BRAND. In God's name – !
GERD. Ssh! Who are you? Stand still, stand still,
  He's flying away.
BRAND. Who is flying away?
GERD. Didn't you see the hawk?
BRAND. Here? No.
GERD. The big ugly bird with the red and gold
  Circled eye?
BRAND. Where are you going?
GERD. To church.
BRAND (*pointing downwards*). But there's the church.
GERD (*smiles scornfully at him, and points downwards*). That?
BRAND. Yes. Come with me.
GERD. No, that's ugly.
BRAND. Ugly? Why?
GERD. Because it's small.
BRAND. Do you know a bigger one?
GERD. A bigger one? Oh, yes. Goodbye. (*Begins to climb.*)
BRAND. Is your church up there? That leads into the mountains.
GERD. Come with me, and I'll show you a church
  Built of ice and snow.
BRAND.   Of ice and snow?

Now I understand. I remember,
When I was a boy, up among the peaks and summits,
At the head of a valley, there was a chasm.
People called it the Ice Church.
A frozen mountain lake was its floor.
And a great piled snowdrift stretched like a roof
Over the split in the mountain wall.
GERD. Yes, it looks like rocks and ice, but really
    It's a church.
BRAND.   Never go there.
    A gust of wind can bring the roof crashing down.
    A scream, a rifle-shot, is enough.
GERD (*not listening*). Come with me, and I'll show you a herd
    Of reindeer which was buried by an avalanche,
    And wasn't seen again till the spring thaw.
BRAND. Don't go there. It's unsafe.
GERD (*pointing down into the valley*).
    Don't go there. It's ugly!
BRAND. God's peace be with you.
GERD.   No, come with me!
    Up there, cataract and avalanche sing Mass.
    The wind preaches along the wall of the glacier,
    And the hawk can't get in; he swoops down
    On to the Black Peak and sits there
    On my church steeple like an ugly weathercock.
BRAND. Wild is your way, and wild your soul,
    Poor, broken instrument.
GERD.   Here he comes
    With his clattering wings; I must get inside.
    Goodbye! In the church, I'm safe.
    Ah! How angry he is! (*Shrieks.*)
    Don't come near me! I'll throw stones at you!
    I'll hit you if you try to claw me.

She runs off up the mountain side.

BRAND (*after a pause*). Another churchgoer!
On the mountain, or in the valley?
Which is best? Who gropes most blindly?
Who strays farthest from home? The light of heart
Who plays along the edge of the crevasse?
The dull of heart, plodding and slow because
His neighbours are so? Or the wild of heart,
In whose broken mind evil seems beautiful?
This triple enemy must be fought.
I see my calling. It shines forth like the sun.
I know my mission. If these three can be slain,
Man's sickness will be cured.
Arm, arm, my soul. Unsheath your sword.
To battle for the heirs of Heaven!

He descends into the valley.

Act Two

Down by the fjord. Steep mountains surround it, and the ruined church stands nearby on a small hill. A storm is building up. VILLAGERS (*men, women and children*) *are gathered in groups on the shore and hillside. In the midst of them, the* MAYOR *is seated on a stone. The* SEXTON *is helping him to dole out corn and other food. Some way off,* EJNAR *and* AGNES *stand surrounded by a group of people. Boats lie on the shingle.*

BRAND *appears on the hill by the church, unnoticed by the crowd.*

A MAN (*forcing his way through the crowd*).
    Get out of the way!
A WOMAN. I was first!
MAN (*pushing her aside*). Make way!
    (*Pushes his way to the* MAYOR.)
    Here, fill my sack!
MAYOR. Be patient.
MAN. I must go home. I've four children starving – five!
MAYOR (*sardonically*). Don't you know how many?
MAN. One was dying when I left.
MAYOR. Well, be patient. You're on the list, I take it?

He glances through his papers.

    No. Yes, here you are. Lucky for you. (*To* SEXTON.)
    Give number twenty-nine his. Now, now, good people,
    Be patient. Nils Snemyr?
SECOND MAN. Yes?
MAYOR. You must take a quarter less than you had last time.
    You've one less mouth to feed.
SECOND MAN. Yes, Ragnhild died yesterday.
MAYOR (*makes a note*). One less. Well, a saving's a saving.

EJNAR (*to* AGNES). I've given all I have – I've emptied
    My pockets and my purse.
MAYOR (*catches sight of* BRAND, *and points up at him*).
    Ha, a new arrival! Welcome!
    We've had drought and famine here, and now floods,
    So open your purse and give what you can.
    We've very little left; five small fishes
    Don't feed many hungry mouths nowadays.
BRAND. Better than ten thousand issued in the name of idolatry.
MAYOR. I didn't ask you for advice.
    Words are no good to hungry men.
EJNAR. Brand, you can't know how the people have suffered.
    The harvest's failed, there's been famine and sickness.
    People are dying –
BRAND. Yes, I can see that. These sunken eyes
    Tell me what judge holds court here.
MAYOR. And yet you stand there hard as stone?
BRAND (*comes down among the crowd, and speaks earnestly*).
    If your life here was languid and easy,
    I could pity your cries for bread. When day follows day
    Ploddingly, like mourners at a funeral,
    Then a man may well suppose that God has struck him
    From His book. But to you He has been merciful,
    He has made you afraid, He has scourged you
    With the whip of death. The precious gift He gave you,
    He has taken away –
SEVERAL VOICES (*threateningly*). He mocks us in our need!
MAYOR. He abuses us who give you bread!
BRAND (*shakes his head*).
    Oh, could my heart's blood heal and refresh you,
    I would pour it till my veins were dry.
    But to help you now would be sin. God
    Shall lift you out of your distress. A living people
    Sucks strength from sorrow. The weak brace their backs,
    Knowing that the strife will end in victory.

But where extremity breeds no courage, the flock
Is not worthy of salvation.

A WOMAN.   A storm is breaking
Over the fjord. His words awake the thunder!

ANOTHER WOMAN. He tempts God!

BRAND. *Your* God will perform no miracles for you!

WOMEN. Look at the sky! The storm is rising!

CROWD. Drive him out of the village! Drive him out!
Stone him! Kill him!

The VILLAGERS *gather threateningly round* BRAND. *The*
MAYOR *tries to intervene.* A WOMAN, *crazed and dishevelled,*
runs down the hillside.

WOMAN (*screams*).
Help me, in the name of Jesus Christ, help me!

MAYOR. What is the matter? What do you want?

WOMAN. A priest, a priest! Where can I find a priest?

MAYOR. We have no priest here.

WOMAN. Then all is lost, lost!

BRAND. Perhaps one could be found.

WOMAN (*clutches his arm*).
Where is he? Tell me! Where is he?

BRAND. Tell me why you need him, and he will come.

WOMAN. Over the fjord – my husband –
Three children, starving – we had no food.
No! Tell me he is not damned!

BRAND. Explain.

WOMAN. My breasts were dry – no one would help us –
God would not help us – my youngest child was dying.
It drove him mad. He killed the child.

CROWD (*fearfully*). Killed his own child!

WOMAN. At once, he realized what he had done.
His grief burst forth like a river, and he turned
His hand on himself. Cross the fjord and save
His soul! He cannot live, and dare not die.

He lies clasping the child's body, shrieking
The Devil's name.

BRAND (*quietly*). Your need is great.

EJNAR (*pale*). Can it be possible?

MAYOR. He doesn't belong to my district.

BRAND (*sharply, to the* VILLAGERS).

Unmoor a boat and row me over.

A MAN. In this storm? No one would dare.

BRAND. Unmoor a boat!

SECOND MAN. Impossible! Look!

The wind's blowing from the mountain! The fjord is
seething!

BRAND. The soul of a dying sinner does not wait
For wind and weather.

He goes to a boat, and unties the sail.

Will you risk your boat?

MAN. Yes, but wait –

BRAND. Good. Now, who will risk his life?

MAN. Not I.

ANOTHER MAN. Nor I.

OTHERS. It's certain death.

BRAND.   Your God will help
No one across. But mine will be on board!

WOMAN. He will die unshriven.

BRAND (*shouts from the boat*). I only need one man,
To bale and work the sail. Come, one of you!
You gave food just now! Won't anyone give his life?

CROWD (*retreating*). You can't ask that!

A MAN (*threateningly*).

Get out of the boat! Don't tempt the Lord!

CROWD. The storm's rising!

BRAND (*holding himself fast with the boathook, shouts to the*
WOMAN). All right, then, you come. But hurry!

WOMAN (*shrinks back*). I? When no one – !

BRAND. Let them stay.

WOMAN. No, I can't.

BRAND. Can't?

WOMAN. My children – !

BRAND (*laughs contemptuously*). You build on sand!

AGNES (*turns with flaming cheeks to* EJNAR, *and lays her hand on his arm*). Did you hear?

EJNAR. Yes. He is strong.

AGNES. God bless you! You know your duty. (*Cries to* BRAND) Here is one who is worthy to go with you.

BRAND. Come on, then.

EJNAR (*pales*). I?

AGNES. Go! I want you to. My eyes were blind; now they see.

EJNAR. A week ago, I would gladly have given my life
And gone with him –

AGNES (*trembling*). But now?

EJNAR. I am young, and life is dear. I cannot go.

AGNES (*draws away from him*). What?

EJNAR. I dare not.

AGNES. This storm has driven us apart.
All God's ocean lies between us now.
(*Cries to* BRAND.) I will come.

BRAND. Good! Come on, then.

WOMEN (*in terror, as she runs on board*).
Help! Jesus Christ have mercy!

EJNAR (*tries desperately to seize her*). Agnes!

CROWD (*rushing forward*). Come back!

BRAND. Where is the house?

WOMAN. Over there, on the headland.

The boat moves away from the shore.

EJNAR (*cries after them*).
Remember your family! Remember your mother!
Save your life!

AGNES. We are three on board!

The boat sails away. The VILLAGERS *gather on the hillside and gaze after them.*

MAN. The squall's caught them!

ANOTHER MAN. The water's boiling like pitch!

EJNAR. What was that cry above the storm?

WOMAN. It came from the mountain.

ANOTHER WOMAN. There! It's the witch, Gerd, laughing
     and shouting at him!

FIRST WOMAN. Blowing a buck's horn, and throwing stones!

SECOND WOMAN. Hooting!

FIRST MAN. Howl and trumpet, you ugly troll! He's well
     protected.

SECOND MAN. Next time he asks, I'll sail with him in a hurri-
     cane.

FIRST MAN (*to* EJNAR). What is he?

EJNAR. A priest.

SECOND MAN. Mm. Well, whatever he is, he's a man.
     Tough and strong. And brave.

FIRST MAN. That's the sort of priest we need.

VILLAGERS. Yes, that's the sort of priest we need.

They look out to sea.

On the headland, outside a hut. The day is far advanced. The fjord lies still and shining. AGNES *is seated down by the shore. After a moment,* BRAND *comes out of the door.*

BRAND. That was death. It has washed away the stains
     Of fear. Now he lies, freed from his pain,
     His face calm and peaceful. But those two children
     Who sat huddled in the chimney corner
     Staring with huge eyes,
     Who only looked and looked, whose souls
     Received a stain which all the toil of time

Will not wash out, even when they themselves
Are bent and grey,
Must grow up in the memory of this hour.
And what chain of sin and crime will not stretch on
From them, link upon link? Why?
The hollow answer echoes: 'They were their father's
Sons'. Silence cannot erase this,
Nor mercy. Where does responsibility
For man's inheritance from man begin?
What a hearing that will be when the great assizes sits!
Who shall bear witness where every man is guilty?
Shall the answer: 'I am my father's son'
Be admitted then?
Deep-dizzy riddle of darkness, which none can solve.
Men do not understand what a mountain of guilt
Rises from that small word: Life.

Some of the VILLAGERS *appear, and approach* BRAND.

FIRST MAN. We meet again.
BRAND. He no longer needs your help.
MAN. There are still three mouths to fill –
BRAND. Well?
MAN. We haven't much to offer, but we've brought a few
       things –
BRAND. If you give all you have, but not your life,
    You give nothing.
MAN. I would give it now, if it could save his life.
BRAND. But not to save his soul?
MAN. We are only working people.
BRAND. Then turn your eyes away from the light
    Beyond the mountains. Bend your backs to the yoke.
MAN. I thought you would tell us to throw it off.
BRAND. Yes, if you can.
MAN. You can give us the strength.

BRAND. Can I?

MAN. Many people have pointed the way, but you
    Walked in it.

BRAND (*uneasily*). What do you want with me?

MAN. Be our priest.

BRAND. I?

MAN. You are the sort of priest we need.

BRAND. Ask anything of me, but not that.
    I have a greater calling. I must speak to the world.
    Where the mountains shut one in, a voice is powerless.
    Who buries himself in a pit when the broad fields beckon?
    Who ploughs the desert when fertile soil awaits him?

MAN (*shakes his head*):
    I understood your deeds, but not your words.

BRAND. Ask no further; my time here is finished. (*Turns to go.*)

MAN. Is your calling dear to you?

BRAND. It is my life.

MAN. If you give all, but not your life,
    You give nothing.

BRAND. One thing a man cannot give: his soul.
    He cannot deny his calling.
    He dare not block that river's course;
    It forces its way towards the ocean.

MAN. Yet if it lost itself in marsh or lake,
    It would reach the ocean in the end, as dew.

BRAND (*looks steadfastly at him*).
    Who gave you power to speak like that?

MAN. You did. In the storm.
    When you risked your life to save a sinner's soul,
    Your deed rang in our ears like a bell. (*Lowers his voice.*)
    Tomorrow, perhaps, we shall have forgotten it.

BRAND. Where there is no will, there is no calling. (*In a hard
    voice.*)
    If you cannot be what you would be,
    Turn your face to the earth, and till it well.

MAN (*looks at him for a moment*).

> May you be cursed for quenching the flame you lit,
> As we are cursed, who, for a moment, saw.

He goes. The others follow him silently.

BRAND (*gazing after him*).

> Silently they go, their spirits bowed,
> As Adam walked from Paradise.
> No! I have dared to take upon myself
> The salvation of Man. That is my work.
> I must leave this narrow valley; I cannot fight
> My battle here.

He turns to go, but stops as he sees AGNES *sitting on the shore.*

> See how she sits and listens, as though the air
> Were full of song. So she sat in the storm. (*Goes towards
>   her*)
> What are you looking at, girl ? The fjord's crooked course ?

AGNES (*without turning*).

> No. Not the fjord's course, nor the earth's.
> Both are hidden from me now.
> But I see a greater earth, its outline
> Sharp against the air.
> I see oceans and the mouths of rivers.
> A gleam of sunshine pierces through the mist.
> I see a fiery red light playing about the mountain peaks.
> I see a boundless waste of desert.
> Great palm trees stand, swaying in the sharp winds.
> There is no sign of life;
> It is like a new world at its birth.
> And I hear voices ring;
> 'Now shalt thou be lost or saved.
> Thy task awaits thee; take up thy burden.
> Thou shalt people this new earth.'

BRAND. What else ?

AGNES (*lays a hand on her breast*).
    I feel a force waking within me;
    And I sense Him who watches over us,
    Sense that He looks down
    Full of sadness and of love.
    A voice cries: 'Now shalt thou create and be created.
    Thy task awaits thee. Take up thy burden.'
BRAND. Yes. Within, within. There is the way,
    That is the path. In oneself is that earth,
    Newly created, ready to receive God.
    There shall the vulture that gnaws the will be slain;
    There shall the new Adam be born.
    A place on the earth where one can be wholly oneself;
    That is Man's right; and I ask no more. (*Reflects for a
        moment.*)
    To be wholly oneself! But how,
    With the weight of one's inheritance of sin?
    Who is that climbing the hill? Who is she –
    Her body crooked and bent?
    What icy gust, what cold memory from childhood
    Numbs me? Merciful God!

BRAND'S MOTHER *climbs over the hilltop and stands there, half
visible, shading her eyes with her hand and peering about her.*

MOTHER. They said he was here. (*Approaches him.*)
    Curse the sun, it half blinds me.
    Is that you, my son?
BRAND. Yes, mother.
MOTHER (*rubs her eyes*).
    Ugh! It's enough to burn one's eyes out.
BRAND. At home I never saw the sun
    From the leaves' fall to the cuckoo's song.
MOTHER (*laughs quietly*). No, it's good there – dark and cold.
    It makes you strong, and afraid of nothing.
BRAND. Good day. My time is short.

MOTHER. Yes, you were always restless; ran away and left me –

BRAND. You wanted me to leave.

MOTHER. It was best. You had to be a priest. (*Looks at him
more closely.*)

Hm! You've grown big and strong. But mark my words.
Take care of your life!

BRAND. Is that all?

MOTHER. All? What could be dearer than life?

Look after yours, for my sake – I gave it to you. (*Angrily.*)
I've heard about your crossing the fjord this morning.
In that storm! You are my only son,
The last of our family. You must live
To carry on my name, and all I've lived
And worked for. You'll be rich, you know, one day.

BRAND. I see. So that's why you came to look for me?

MOTHER. Keep away! (*Draws back.*) Don't come near me!

I'll hit you with my stick! (*More calmly.*) Listen to me.
I'm getting older every year. Sooner or later
I've got to die, and then you'll get all I have.
It's not much, but it's enough.
You shall have it all, my son. The whole inheritance.

BRAND. On what conditions?

MOTHER. Only one. That you don't throw your life away.

Pass on our name to sons and grandsons.
That's all I ask.

BRAND.   Let's be clear about one thing.

I have always defied you, even when I was a child.
I have been no son to you, and you have been
No mother to me.

MOTHER.   I don't ask for sentiment.

Be what you want – be hard, be stubborn, be cold –
I shan't weep. But guard your inheritance.
Never let it leave our family.

BRAND (*takes a step towards her*).

And if I should decide to scatter it to the winds?

MOTHER. Scatter it?

    The money I've drudged all my life to save?

BRAND (*nodding slowly*). Scatter it to the winds.

MOTHER. If you do, you scatter my soul with it.

BRAND. But if I should?

    If I should come to your bedside one evening,
    When a candle stands at the foot of your bed;
    When, clasping a psalmbook in your hands,
    You lie, sleeping your first night with death –

MOTHER (*goes towards him tensely*). Who gave you this idea?

BRAND. Shall I tell you?

MOTHER. Yes.

BRAND. A memory from childhood. Something
    I cannot forget. It was an autumn evening.
    Father was dead. I crept in to where he lay
    Pale in the candlelight. I stood
    And stared at him from a corner. He was holding
    A psalmbook. I wondered why he slept so deeply,
    And why his wrists were so thin; and I remember
    The smell of clammy linen. Then I heard
    A step on the stair. A woman came in.
    She didn't see me, but went straight to the bed,
    And began to grope and rummage. She moved the head
    And pulled out a bundle; then another. She counted,
    And whispered: 'More, more!' Then she pulled out
    From the pillows a packet bound with cord,
    She tore, she fumbled at it with greedy fingers,
    She bit it open with her teeth, searched on,
    Found more, counted, and whispered: 'More, more!'
    She wept, she prayed, she wailed, she swore.
    At last she had emptied every hiding-place.
    She slunk out of the room like a damned soul,
    Groaning: 'So this was all!'

MOTHER. I needed the money; and God knows
    There was precious little. I paid dearly enough for it.

BRAND. Yes, dearly. It cost you your son.

MOTHER. Maybe. But I paid a bigger price than that.
    I think I gave my life. I gave something
    Which is dead now; something foolish and beautiful.
    I gave – I hardly know what it was –
    People called it love. I remember
    What a hard struggle it was. I remember
    My father's advice. 'Forget the village boy',
    He said, 'Take the other. Never mind that he's old
    And withered. He's clever. He'll double his money.'
    I took him, and it only brought me shame.
    He never doubled his money. But I've worked
    And slaved since then, so that now I'm not so poor.

BRAND. And do you remember, now you are near your grave,
    That you gave your soul, too?

MOTHER. I remember. But I made my son a priest.
    When my time comes, you must look after my soul,
    In return for your inheritance.

BRAND.   And the debt?

MOTHER. Debt? What debt? I won't leave any debts.

BRAND. But if you should? I must answer every claim.
    That is a son's duty when his mother
    Is laid in her grave.

MOTHER.   There's no such law.

BRAND. Not in the statutes; but it must be obeyed.
    Blind woman, learn to see! You have debased
    God's coinage, you have squandered the soul He lent you,
    You were born in His image, and you
    Have dragged it in the mire. That is your debt.
    Where will you go when God demands His own?

MOTHER (*timidly*). Where shall I go? Where?

BRAND. Have no fear. Your son
    Takes all your debt on him. God's corroded image
    Shall be burnt clean in me. Go to your death
    In comfort. My mother shall not sleep debt-bound.

MOTHER. And my sins?

BRAND. No; only your debt; you yourself must answer
    For your sins. You must repent or perish.

MOTHER (*uneasily*). I'd better go back home
    Under the shadow of the glacier.
    In this hot glare, rank thoughts sprout like weeds.
    The stench is enough to make you giddy.

BRAND. Go back to your shadows. I am near.
    If you feel drawn towards the light
    And wish to see me, send, and I will come.

MOTHER. Yes, to judge me.

BRAND.   No, as a son
    To love you, and as a priest to shrive you.
    I shall shield you against the chill wind
    Of fear. I shall sit at the foot of your bed
    And cool the burning in your blood with song.

MOTHER. Do you promise that?

BRAND. I shall come in the hour of your repentance. (*Goes
        closer to her.*)
    But I, too, make one condition.
    Everything that binds you to this world
    You must renounce, and go naked to your grave.

MOTHER. Ask anything else! Not what I love most!

BRAND. Nothing less can mitigate His judgment.

MOTHER. My life wasted, my soul lost,
    And soon my life's savings will be lost too.
    I'll go home then,
    And hug the little I can still call mine.
    My treasure, my child of pain,
    For you I tore my breast until it bled.
    I will go home and weep like a mother
    At the cradle of her sick child.
    Why was my soul made flesh
    If love of the flesh is death to the soul?
    Stay near me, priest. I don't know how I shall feel

When my time is near. If I must lose everything
At least let me keep it as long as I can.

Goes.

BRAND (*looking after her*).
    Your son will stay near, to answer your call.
    And if you stretch your withered, freezing hand,
    He will warm it. (*Goes down to* AGNES.) This evening
    Is not as the morning was. Then I was eager
    For battle. I heard distant trumpets bray,
    And longed to swing the sword of wrath
    To kill the demon of untruth,
    Filling the earth with the noise of war.
AGNES (*turns, and looks up at him with shining eyes*).
    The morning was pale; but the evening glows.
    This morning I laughed; my laughter was a lie.
    I lived for that the loss whereof is gain.
BRAND. This morning visions flocked to me
    Like wild swans, and lifted me on their broad wings.
    I looked outwards, thinking my path lay there.
    I saw myself as the chastiser of the age,
    Striding in greatness above the tumult.
    The pomp of processions, hymns
    And incense, silken banners, golden cups,
    Songs of victory, the acclaim
    Of surging crowds, glorified my life's work.
    But it was an empty dream, a mountain mirage
    Made by the sun in the morning mist.
    Now I stand in a deep valley, where darkness
    Falls long before evening. I stand between
    The mountain and the sea, far from the tumult
    Of the world. But this is my home.
    My Sunday song is over, my winged steed
    Can be unsaddled. My duty lies here.

There is a higher purpose than the glory of battle.
To hallow daily toil to the praise of God.

AGNES. And that God who was to fall?

BRAND.   I shall bury him.
But secretly, in each man's soul, not openly
For all to see. I thought I knew the way
To cure man's sickness, but I was wrong.
I see it now.
It is not by spectacular achievements
That man can be transformed, but by will.
It is man's will that acquits or condemns him.

*He turns towards the village, where the evening shadows are
beginning to fall.*

You men who wander dully in this damp
Hill-locked valley which is my home. Let us see
If we can become tablets on which God can write.

He is about to go, when EJNAR *appears, and stops him.*

EJNAR. Stop! Give me back what you took from me.

BRAND. Her? There she sits.

EJNAR (*to* AGNES). Choose between the sunny plains and this
        dark corner of sorrow.

AGNES. I have no choice.

EJNAR. Agnes, Agnes, listen to me.
        Out on the shining water, the white sails
        Cut from the shore, the high prows pearled with spray.
        They fly towards harbour in our promised land.

AGNES. Sail west or east, but think of me as one dead.
        Go, and God be with you, fair tempter.

EJNAR. Agnes, come with me as a sister.

AGNES (*shakes her head*). All God's ocean lies between us.

EJNAR. Then come home with me to your mother.

AGNES (*calmly*). He is my teacher, my brother and my friend.
        I shall not leave him.

BRAND (*takes a step towards them*).

    Young woman, think carefully before you decide.

    Locked between mountain and mountain, shadowed by
        crag

    And peak, shut in the twilight of this ravine,

    My life will flow like a sad October evening.

AGNES. The darkness no longer frightens me. A star

    Pierces through the night.

BRAND.   Remember, I am stern

    In my demands. I require All or Nothing.

    No half-measures. There is no forgiveness

    For failure. It may not be enough

    To offer your life. Your death may be required also.

EJNAR. Stop this mad game, leave this man of dark law.

    Live the life you know you can.

BRAND. Choose. You stand at the parting of the ways.

EJNAR. Choose between storm and calm,

    Choose between joy and sorrow, night and morning.

    Choose between death and life.

AGNES (*rises*). Into the night; through death.

    Beyond, the morning glows.

She goes after BRAND. EJNAR *stares after her for a moment as
though lost, bows his head, and turns back towards the fjord.*

Act Three

Three years later. A small garden at the parsonage. High mountains tower above it; a stone wall surrounds it. The fjord is visible in the background, narrow and mountain-locked. The door of the house leads into the garden. It is afternoon.

BRAND *is standing on the step outside the house.* AGNES *is seated on the step below him.*

AGNES. My dearest husband, again your eye travels anxiously
　　Along the fjord.
BRAND. 　　　　　　I am waiting for a message.
AGNES. You are uneasy.
BRAND. I am waiting for a message from my mother.
　　For three years I have waited faithfully,
　　But it has never come. This morning
　　I heard for certain that her hour is near.
AGNES (*quiet and loving*).
　　Brand, you ought to go to her without waiting
　　For any message.
BRAND (*shakes his head*). If she does not repent,
　　I have no words to say to her, no comfort
　　To offer her.
AGNES. 　　　　She is your mother.
BRAND. I have no right to worship gods in my family.
AGNES. You are hard, Brand.
BRAND. Towards you?
AGNES. Oh, no!
BRAND. I told you it would be a hard life.
AGNES (*smiles*).
　　It has not been so; you have not kept your word.
BRAND. Yes; this place is cold and bitter. The rose
　　Has faded from your cheek; your gentle spirit freezes.

The sun never warms this house.

AGNES. It dances so warmly and mildly on the shoulder
　Of the mountain opposite.

BRAND.　　　　　　　　　For three weeks
　In the summer. But it never reaches the valley.

AGNES (*looks steadily at him, and rises to her feet*).
　Brand, there is something you are afraid of.

BRAND. I? No, you.

AGNES. No, Brand. You.

BRAND. You have a secret fear.

AGNES. So have you.

BRAND. You tremble, as though on the edge of a precipice.
　What is it? Tell me.

AGNES. Sometimes I have trembled – (*Stops.*)

BRAND. For whom?

AGNES. For our son.

BRAND. For Ulf?

AGNES. You have, too?

BRAND. Yes, sometimes. No, no!
　He cannot be taken from us. God is good.
　My son will grow well and strong. Where is he now?

AGNES. Sleeping.

BRAND (*looks in through the door*).
　Look at him; he does not dream of sickness
　Or sorrow. His little hand is round and plump.

AGNES. But pale.

BRAND. Pale, yes. But that will pass.

AGNES. How peacefully he sleeps.

BRAND. God bless you, my son. Sleep soundly. (*Closes the door.*)
　You and he have given me light and peace
　In my work. You have made every moment of sorrow,
　Every difficult task, easy to bear.
　Your courage has never failed me; his childish play
　Gives me strength.
　I thought my calling would be a martyrdom,

But success has followed me on my journey.

AGNES. Yes, Brand, but you deserve success.

You have fought and suffered, have toiled and drudged.

I know you have wept blood silently.

BRAND. Yes, but it all seemed easy to me. With you

Love came like a sunny spring day to warm my heart.

I had never known it before. My father and mother

Never loved me. They quenched any little flame

That faltered from the ashes. It was as though

All the gentleness I carried suppressed within me

Had been saved so that I could give it all to you

And him.

AGNES.   Not only to us. To others too.

BRAND. Through you and him. You taught me

Gentleness of spirit. That was the bridge to their hearts.

No one can love all until he has first loved one.

AGNES. And yet your love is hard.

Where you would caress, you bruise.

Many have shrunk from us, at your demand

Of: All or Nothing.

BRAND. What the world calls love, I neither know nor want.

I know God's love, which is neither weak nor mild.

It is hard, even unto the terror of death;

Its caress is a scourge. What did God reply

In the olive grove when His Son lay in agony

And cried, and prayed: 'Take this cup from me'?

Did He take the cup of pain from his lips?

No child; he had to drink it to the dregs.

AGNES. Measured by that yardstick, we all stand condemned.

BRAND. No man knows whom the judgment shall touch.

But it stands written in eternal letters of fire:

'Be steadfast to the end!' It is not enough

To bathe in the sweat of anguish; you must pass

Through the fire of torture. That you *cannot*

Will be forgiven; that you *will* not, never.

AGNES. Yes, it must be so. Oh, lift me, lift me
    To where you climb. Lead me towards your high heaven.
    My longing is great, my courage weak.
    I grow dizzy, my feet are tired
    And clogged with earth.

BRAND. Listen, Agnes. There is but one law
    For all men: no cowardly compromise!
    If a man does his work by halves,
    He stands condemened.

AGNES (*throws her arms round his neck*).
    Lead, and I shall follow.

BRAND. No path is too steep for two to climb.

The DOCTOR *comes down the path and stops outside the garden
wall.*

DOCTOR. Hullo, I never expected to see
    Lovebirds in this cold valley.

AGNES. Dear doctor, are you here? Come in!

She runs down and opens the garden gate.

DOCTOR. No, I won't! You know quite well
    I'm angry with you! Burying yourselves
    In this damp cellar, where the wind from the mountain
    Cuts through body and soul like a knife.

BRAND. Not through the soul

DOCTOR. No? Well – no, it almost seems so. Well,
    I must be off – I've got to visit a patient.

BRAND. My mother?

DOCTOR. Yes. Care to come with me?

BRAND. Not now.

DOCTOR. You've been to see her already, perhaps?

BRAND. No.

DOCTOR. You're a hard man. I've struggled all the way
    Across the moor, through mist and sleet,
    Although I know she pays like a pauper.

BRAND. May God bless your energy and skill.
 Ease her suffering, if you can.

DOCTOR. I hope He may bless my sense of duty.
 I came as soon as I heard she needed me.

BRAND. She sends for you; I am forgotten.
 I wait, wait.

DOCTOR. Don't wait for her to send for you. Come now, with
  me.

BRAND. Until she sends for me, I know no duty there.

DOCTOR (*to* AGNES). Poor child, you have a hard master.

BRAND. I am not hard.

AGNES. He would give his blood if it could wash her soul.

BRAND. As her son, I shall pay her debts.
 They are my inheritance.

DOCTOR. Pay your own!

BRAND. One man may pay for the sins of many.

DOCTOR. Not when he himself is a beggar.

BRAND. Whether I am rich or a beggar, I have the will;
 That is enough.

DOCTOR (*looks sternly at him*).
 Yes, in your ledger your credit account
 For strength of will is full, but, priest,
 Your love account is a white virgin page.

He goes.

BRAND (*watching him go*).
 Love! Has any word been so abused
 And debased? It is used as a veil to cover weakness.
 When the path is narrow, steep and slippery,
 It can be cut short – by love.
 When a man walks on the broad road of sin,
 There is still hope – in love.
 When he sees his goal but will not fight towards it,
 He can conquer – through love.
 When he goes astray, knowing what is right,

He may yet find refuge in love!

AGNES. Yes, love is a snare. And yet –
I sometimes wonder – is it?

BRAND. First there must be will.
You must will your way through fear, resolutely,
Joyfully. It is not
Martyrdom to die in agony on a cross;
But to *will* that you shall die upon a cross,
To will it in the extremity of pain,
To will it when the spirit cries in torment,
That is to find salvation.

AGNES (*clings to him*).
Oh, Brand. When the path becomes too steep for me,
You must give me strength.

BRAND. When the will has triumphed, then comes the time for
        love.
But here, faced by a generation
Which is lax and slothful, the best love is hate. (*In terror.*)
Hate! Hate! But to will that simple word
Means universal war.

He rushes into the house.

AGNES. He kneels by the child; he rocks his head
As though he wept. He presses himself
Against the cot like a man desperate for comfort.
What a deep well of love exists in his soul!
He can love his child; the snake of human weakness
Has not yet bitten that small heart.

BRAND (*comes out on to the steps*). Has no message come?

AGNES. No, no message.

BRAND (*looks back into the house*).
His skin is dry and hot, his temple throbs,
His pulse beats fast. Don't be afraid, Agnes –

AGNES. Oh, God!

BRAND. No, don't be afraid. (*Shouts down the road.*) The
          message! At last!
A MAN (*through the garden gate*).
          Father, you must come now!
BRAND (*eagerly*). At once! What message does she send?
MAN. A strange message. She raised herself in bed,
          Leaned forward, and said: 'Bring the priest,
          I will give half my goods for the sacrament.'
BRAND. Half!
MAN. Half.
BRAND. Half? Half! She meant all!
MAN. Maybe; but I heard her clearly.
BRAND (*seizes him by the arm*).
          Dare you swear, on the day of judgment,
          That she used that word?
MAN. Yes.
BRAND (*sternly*). Go and say that this is my reply.
          No priest will come; no sacrament.
MAN. You can't have understood. Your mother sent me.
BRAND. I know but one law for all mankind.
          I cannot discriminate.
MAN. Those are hard words.
BRAND. She knows what she must offer: All or Nothing.
MAN. Priest!
BRAND. Say that the least fragment of the golden
          Calf is as much an idol as the whole.
MAN. I will give her your answer as gently as I can.
          She'll have one comfort: God is not as hard as you.

          He goes.

BRAND. Yes; they always comfort themselves
          With that illusion. A psalm and a few tears
          Just before the end, and all will be forgiven.
          Of course! They know their old God; they know
          He is always ready to be bargained with.

The MAN *has met a* SECOND MAN *on the path. They return together.*

BRAND. Another message?
FIRST MAN. Yes.
BRAND. Tell me.
SECOND MAN. She says she will give nine-tenths of her wealth.
BRAND. Not all?
SECOND MAN. No.
BRAND. She knows my answer: no priest, no sacrament.
SECOND MAN. She begged – in pain!
FIRST MAN. Priest, remember – she gave you birth!
BRAND. Go and tell her:
    'The table for the bread and wine must be clean.'

    The MEN *go.*

AGNES (*clings tightly to him*).
    Brand, sometimes you frighten me. You flame
    Like the sword of God.
BRAND (*with tears in his voice*). Does not the world fight me
    With its stubborn apathy?
AGNES.   Your terms are hard.
BRAND. What other terms would you dare offer?
AGNES. Could anyone meet them?
BRAND. No, you are right. So false,
    So empty, so flat, so mean has man become.
AGNES. And yet, from this blind, stumbling generation,
    You demand: All or Nothing?
BRAND. He who seeks victory must not weaken;
    He who has sunk most low may rise most high.

He is silent for a moment; when he speaks again, it is with a changed voice.

    And yet, when I stand before a simple man
    And make that demand, I feel as though I were floating

In a storm-wracked sea on a shattered spar.
Go, Agnes, go in to the child.
Sing to him, and give him sweet dreams.

AGNES (*pale*).

What is it, Brand? Your thoughts always return to him.

BRAND. Oh, nothing. Take good care of him.

AGNES. Give me a text.

BRAND. Stern?

AGNES. No, gentle.

BRAND (*embracing her*). He who is without stain shall live.

AGNES (*looks up at him with shining eyes*). Yes!

There is one sacrifice which God dare not demand.

He goes into the house.

BRAND. But if He should dare? If He should test me
    As He tested Abraham?

MAYOR (*over the garden gate*). Good afternoon.

BRAND. Ah, his worship the Mayor.

MAYOR. We don't see each other often.
    So I thought – but perhaps this is a bad time?

BRAND (*indicates the house*). Come in.

MAYOR. Thank you.

BRAND. What do you want?

MAYOR. Your mother's sick, I hear; very sick.
    I'm sorry to hear that.

BRAND. I don't doubt it.

MAYOR. *Very* sorry.

BRAND. What do you want?

MAYOR. Well, I – er – I've a little suggestion to make.
    I hope you don't mind my broaching the subject
    At this sad time?

BRAND. Now is as good as any other time.

MAYOR. Well, I'll come straight to the point. You're going
    To be quite well off now – I may even say rich.
    You won't want to bury yourself in this little

Backwater any longer, I presume,
Now that you have the means to live elsewhere?

BRAND. In other words: go?

MAYOR. If you like to put it that way.
I think it would be better for all concerned.
Don't misunderstand me! I admire your gifts
Greatly, but wouldn't they be better suited
To a more sophisticated community?

BRAND. A man's native soil is to him as the root
Is to the tree. If he is not wanted there,
His work is doomed, his song dies.

MAYOR. If you insist on staying, of course I can't force you
to go.
But don't overstep the limits of your calling.

BRAND. A man must be himself.
Only thus can he carry his cause to victory.
And I shall carry mine to victory.
This people whom you and your like have lulled
To sleep shall be awakened. You have softened
And debased the good metal of their souls.
I declare war on you and everything
You stand for.

MAYOR.   War?

BRAND.   War.

MAYOR. If you sound the call to arms, you will be
The first to fall.

BRAND.   One day it will be clear
That the greatest victory lies in defeat.

MAYOR. Think, Brand. If you stay,
And lose this battle, your life will have been wasted.
You have all the good things of the world –
Money, a child, a wife who loves you. Why
Wage your crusade in this backwater?

BRAND. Because I must.

MAYOR. Go to rich cities where life is not so hard,

And order them to bleed. We do not want to bleed
But only to earn our bread in the sweat of our brows,
Prising a living out of these rocky hillsides.

BRAND. I shall stay here. This is my home, and here
I shall begin my war.

MAYOR. You're throwing away a great opportunity.
And remember what you stand to lose if you should fail.

BRAND. I lose myself if I weaken.

MAYOR. Brand, no man can fight a war alone.

BRAND. My flock is strong. I have the best men on my side.

MAYOR (*smiles*). Possibly. But I have the most.

He goes.

BRAND (*watching him go*).
There goes a typical man of the people;
Full-blooded, right-thinking, well-meaning, energetic,
Jovial and just. And yet, no landslide, flood
Or hurricane, no famine, frost or plague
Does half the damage in a year that that man does.
How much spiritual aspiration
Has he not stifled at birth? (*Suddenly anxious.*)
Why does no message come? Ah, doctor! (*Runs to meet him.*)
Tell me – my mother – ?

DOCTOR. She stands before her judge.

BRAND. Dead? But – penitent?

DOCTOR. I hardly think so. She clung fast
To her worldly goods until God took her from them.

BRAND. What did she say?

DOCTOR. She mumbled: God is not so cruel as my son.

BRAND (*sinks down on the bench*).
That lie that poisons every soul, even
At the threshold of death, even in the hour of judgment.

He buries his face in his hands.

DOCTOR (*goes close to him, looks at him and shakes his head*).
    You want to resurrect an age that is dead.
    You still preach the pact Jehovah
    Made with man five thousand years ago.
    Every generation must make its own pact with God.
    Our generation is not to be scared by rods
    Of fire, or by nurses' tales about damned souls.
    Its first commandment, Brand, is: Be humane.
BRAND (*looks up at him*). Humane! That word excuses all our
    weakness.
    Was God humane towards Jesus Christ?

He hides his head and sits in silent grief.

DOCTOR (*quietly*). If only you could find tears!
AGNES (*comes out on to the step; pale and frightened she whispers
    to the* DOCTOR).
    Come inside. Please.
DOCTOR. What is it, child?
AGNES. I am afraid.
DOCTOR. What? Why?
AGNES (*takes him by the hand*). Come!

They go into the house, unnoticed by BRAND.

BRAND (*quietly to himself*).
    She died unrepentant; unrepentant
    As she had lived. Is not this God's finger pointing?
    If I weaken now, I am damned tenfold. (*Gets up.*)
    Henceforth I shall fight unflinchingly for the victory
    Of the spirit over the weakness of the flesh.
    The Lord has armed me with the blade of His word;
    He has inflamed me with the fire of His wrath.
    Now I stand strong in my will;
    Now I dare, now I can, crush mountains.

The DOCTOR *comes hurriedly out on to the steps, followed by*
AGNES.

DOCTOR. Put your affairs in order and leave this place.
BRAND. If the earth trembled, I would still remain.
DOCTOR. Then your child will die.
BRAND (*uncomprehendingly*). My child! Ulf? My child?

He rushes towards the house.

DOCTOR (*restraining him*). No, wait!
    Listen to me! There's no light or sunshine here.
    The wind cuts like a polar blast;
    The clammy mist never lifts. The child is weak;
    Another winter here will kill him.
    Go, Brand, and your son will live.
    But do it quickly. Tomorrow, if you can.
BRAND. Tonight – today – now.
    Come, Agnes, lift him gently in his sleep.
    Let us fly south. Oh Agnes, Agnes,
    Death is spinning its web about our child.
    Wrap him warmly; it will soon be evening,
    And the wind is cold.

    AGNES *goes into the house.*

The DOCTOR *watches* BRAND *silently as he stands motionless,
staring in through the door. Then he goes up to him, and places a
hand on his shoulder.*

DOCTOR. So merciless towards your flock, so lenient towards
        yourself.
BRAND. What do you mean?
DOCTOR. You threatened your mother: 'Unless you renounce
        everything
    And go naked to your grave, you are lost.'
    Now you are the shipwrecked soul clinging
    To your upturned boat, overboard now
    Go all your threats of damnation. You fly south,
    Away from your flock and your calling.
    The priest will not preach here again.

BRAND (*clasps his head in his hands' distraught*).
    Am I blind now? Or was I blind before?
DOCTOR. You act as a father should. Don't think I blame you.
    I find you bigger now with your wings clipped
    Than when you were the Angel of God. Goodbye.
    I have given you a mirror; look at it, and ask yourself:
    'Is this a man who would storm the gates of Heaven?'

    He goes.

BRAND (*is silent for a moment, then cries suddenly*).
    Was I wrong then, or am I now?

AGNES *comes out of the door with her cloak over her shoulders
and the child in her arms.* BRAND *does not see her. She is about
to speak to him, but stands as though numbed by fear as she sees
the expression on his face.* A MAN *rushes in through the garden
gate. The sun is setting.*

MAN. Father, father, listen to me. You've an enemy.
BRAND (*puts his hand on his heart*). Yes, here.
MAN. Be on your guard against the mayor.
    He's spreading rumours. He's saying the parsonage
    Will soon be empty, that you will turn your back on us
    Now that your rich mother is dead.
BRAND. And if I did?
MAN. Then – you've been lying to us all!
BRAND. Have I?
MAN. How many times haven't you told us that God
    Sent you here to fight for us? That it's better
    For a man to die than to betray his calling?
    This is your calling, here, among us.
BRAND. Here the people are deaf. Their hearts are dead.
MAN. You know better. You've shown us the light.
BRAND. For every one who has found the light, ten remain in
        darkness.
MAN. I am that one; and I say to you:

'Go if you can!' I can't help myself
From the book; you have dragged me up from the abyss.
See if you dare let me fall! You can't!
If you let me go, my soul is lost. Goodbye.
I am not afraid. My priest and my God will not fail me.

He goes.

BRAND. Every word I say echoes back at me
    Like thunder from the mountain wall.
AGNES (*takes a step towards him*). I am ready.
BRAND. Ready? For what?
AGNES. To go.

   GERD *runs down the path and stops outside the garden gate.*

GERD (*claps her hands and shouts gleefully*). Have you heard?
       The parson's flown away!
    The trolls and demons are swarming out of the hillsides,
    Black and ugly. Big ones, small ones – oh!
    How sharply they can strike! They nearly
    Tore my eye out. They've taken half my soul.
    But I can manage with what's left.
BRAND. Child, you talk crazily. Look at me; I am still here.
GERD. You? Yes, you, but not the priest.
    My hawk swept down the mountainside
    From Black Peak. Bridled, saddled, wild and angry,
    Hissing down the evening wind. And on his back
    A man rode. The priest, it was the priest!
    The village church stands empty, locked and barred.
    Its time is up; it's ugly.
    My church's time has come now. There stands my priest,
    Big and strong, in his white cloak woven of ice.
    Come along with me!
BRAND. Stricken soul, who sent you to bewilder me
    With talk of idols?

GERD (*comes in through the gate*).

> Idols? There's one, do you see him?
> See those hands and feet under the blanket.
> Man, there's an idol!

BRAND. Agnes, Agnes!

> I fear a Greater One has sent her to us.

GERD. Can you see the thousand trolls

> The village priest drowned in the sea?
> That grave can't hold them; they're groping their way
>   ashore,
> Cold and slimy. Look at the troll children!
> They're only skin-dead; see how they grin
> As they push up the rocks that pinned them down.

BRAND. Get out of my sight!

GERD. Listen! Can you hear that one laughing

> As he sits astride the crosspoint where the road
> Swings up to the moor, writing down in his book
> The name of every soul that passes? He has them all.
> The old church stands empty, locked and barred.
> The priest flew away on the hawk's back.

She leaps over the gate and disappears among the rocks. Silence.

AGNES (*goes across to* BRAND; *says quietly*). Let us go, Brand.
>   It is time.

BRAND (*stares at her*). Which way? (*Points towards the gate, then
>   towards the door of the house.*)

> That way – or that?

AGNES. Brand! Your child, your child!

BRAND. Answer me;

> Was I not a priest before I was a father?

AGNES. I cannot answer.

BRAND. You must. You are the mother.

AGNES. I am your wife. I shall do as you command me.

BRAND. I cannot choose! Take this cup from me!

AGNES. Ask yourself if you have a choice.

BRAND (*seizes her hand*). You must choose, Agnes.

AGNES. Do as your God bids you.

Silence.

BRAND. Let us go. It is late.

AGNES (*tonelessly*). Which way? (BRAND *is silent. She points towards the gate.*)

That way?

BRAND (*points towards the door of the house*). No. That.

AGNES (*lifts the child high in her arms*).

Oh, God! This sacrifice You dare demand
I dare to raise towards Your heaven.
Lead me through the fire of life.

She goes into the house.

BRAND (*stands staring silently for a moment, then bursts into tears and throws himself down on the step*).

Jesus! Jesus! Give me light!

Act Four

In the parsonage. It is Christmas Eve. In the rear wall is the front door of the house; in one side wall is a window, in the other is another door.

AGNES, dressed in mourning, is standing at the window, staring out into the darkness.

AGNES. Still no sign of him. No sign.
  Oh, how hard it is to wait
  Listening to the silence. The snow falls soft and thick,
  Binding the church in a tight shroud. (*Listens.*)
  Ssh! I hear the gate creak.
  Footsteps. (*Runs to the door and opens it.*)
  Is it you? Come in, come in.

BRAND enters, covered in snow. He begins to take off his travelling clothes.

AGNES (*embraces him*). Oh, how long you've been away.
      Don't leave me,
  Don't leave me. I cannot shake off
  The black shadows of night alone.
BRAND. You have me back now, child.

He lights a single candle, which illumines the room feebly.

                                        You are pale.

AGNES. I am tired. I have watched and yearned.
  I've bound some branches together, just a few;
  It was all I had saved
  From the summer, to decorate the Christmas tree.
  His branches, I called them, because he liked
  Their leaves. He had some of them for his wreath.

She bursts into tears.

Look, it is half covered with snow,
In the –
BRAND. In the graveyard.
AGNES. That word!
BRAND. Dry your tears.
AGNES. Yes, I will. But be patient.
My soul still bleeds, the wound is fresh,
I have no strength. It will be better soon.
BRAND. Is this how you honour Our Lord's birthday?
AGNES. I know, Brand. But give me time, you must give me
time.
Think, last Christmas he was so well and strong,
And now he –
BRAND (*sharply*). Lies in the graveyard.
AGNES (*screams*). Don't say it!
BRAND. It must be said. Shouted – if you are afraid of it.
AGNES. It frightens you more than you will admit.
Your brow is wet. I know what it cost you to say it.
BRAND. It is only the spray from the fjord.
AGNES. And what is that in your eyes? Melted snow?
No, it is warm.
BRAND.   Agnes, we must both be strong.
We must strengthen each other, fight our way
Step by step together. Out on the fjord
An hour ago, I was a man. The water
Seethed around us, the mast shook,
Our sail was slit and blew far to leeward,
Every nail in the boat screeched,
Rocks were falling on either side from the slopes.
My eight men sat at their oars like corpses,
But I exulted in it. I grew stronger.
I took command. I knew
A Great One had baptized me to my calling.

AGNES. It is easy to be strong in the storm,
      Easy to live the warrior's life.
      But to sit alone in silence, nursing one's grief,
      Performing dull and humble tasks, is harder.
      I am afraid to remember, yet I cannot forget.
BRAND. Your task is not small or humble, Agnes.
      It was never as great as it is now.
      Listen. I want to tell you something
      That has come to me in our sorrow.
      It is as though there lay a kind of joy
      In being able to weep – to weep!
      Agnes, then I see God closer
      Than I ever saw Him before.
      O, so near that it seems as though I might touch Him,
      And I thirst to cast myself into His bosom,
      To be sheltered by His strong, loving, fatherly arms.
AGNES. O Brand, always see Him so,
      As a God you can approach,
      More like a father, less like a master.
BRAND. I must see Him great and strong,
      As great as Heaven. I must fight
      In the heat of the day, keep watch through the cold night.
      You must give me love. Your task is not small.
AGNES. Brand, last night, when you were away,
      He came into my room, rosy-cheeked,
      Dressed in his little shirt; tottered
      Towards my bed, and stretched out his arms,
      Smiled, and called: 'Mother', but as though he were asking
      To be warmed. I saw it – oh! I shivered –
BRAND. Agnes!
AGNES. Yes. The child was freezing.
      He must be cold out there, under the snow.
BRAND. His body is under the snow, but the child is in heaven.
AGNES. Why do you tear open the wound?
      What you call his body is still my child to me.

I cannot separate the two.

BRAND. Your wound must remain open and bleed,
Before it can be healed.

AGNES. Yes, but you must be patient. I can be led,
But not driven. Stay near me, Brand.
Give me strength. Speak to me gently.
The God you taught me to know is a warrior God.
How dare I go to Him with my small sorrow?

BRAND. Would you have found it easier to have turned
To the God you worshipped before?

AGNES. No. I shall never turn to that God again.
And yet sometimes
I long to be where light and sunshine are.
Your kingdom is too big for me. Everything here
Is too big for me; you, your calling,
This mountain that hangs over us, our grief,
Our memories. Only the church is too small.

BRAND. The church? Why is it too small?

AGNES. I can't explain it. I feel it. The church is too small.

BRAND. Many people have said the same to me.
Even the mad girl I met on the moor
Said it. 'The church is ugly
Because it is too small', she screamed.
She couldn't explain either. Many women
Have said it since. 'Our village church is too small.'
Agnes! You can find the right road blindfold
Where I pass by the turning.
Our Lord's church is small. Well, it must be rebuilt.
Again you guide me. You see how much I need you.
It is I who say to you. 'Do not leave me, Agnes.'

AGNES. I shall shake off my sorrow, I will dry my tears.
I will bury my memories. I will be wholly your wife.

She turns to go.

BRAND. Where are you going?

AGNES (*smiles*). I must not forget my household duties,
  Least of all tonight. Do you remember
  Last Christmas you said I was wasteful, because
  I had a candle burning in every window;
  Green branches and pretty things,
  Toys on the Christmas tree, singing and laughter?
  Brand, this year I shall put lights everywhere
  Again, to remind us that it is Christmas.
  I shall make the house as bright as I can
  For Christ's birthday. Now do you see any tears in my
   eyes?

BRAND (*embraces her*).
  Light the candles, child. That is your task.

AGNES (*smiles sadly*).
  Build your big church. But have it built by the spring.

She goes.

BRAND. O God, give her strength. Take from me the cup,
  The bitterest cup, of bending her to Thy law.
  I have strength. I have courage.
  Lay upon me a double portion of Thy load.
  Only be merciful unto her.

A knock upon the door. The MAYOR *enters.*

MAYOR. Well, you've beaten me.

BRAND. Beaten you?

MAYOR. Yes. I reckoned I'd beat you, father.
  Well, I proved a bad prophet.

BRAND. Well?

MAYOR. I'm in the right. But I shan't fight you any longer.

BRAND. Why?

MAYOR. Because you've got the people on your side.

BRAND. Have I?

MAYOR. You know that. And no man's fool enough
  To fight a war alone.

BRAND. Well, what do you intend to do?

MAYOR. I'm going to build.

BRAND. Build, did you say?

MAYOR. Yes. For my own sake.
    As well as for the village. Election time
    Will soon be here, and I must show the people
    That I have their best interests at heart.
    Otherwise they may elect some worthless fellow
    In my place. So I thought I'd discuss with you
    What would be the best measures to improve
    The welfare of our poor parishioners.

BRAND. You want to abolish poverty?

MAYOR. Certainly not. Poverty's a necessity
    In every society; we've got to accept that.
    But with a little skill it can be kept
    Within limits, and moulded into decent forms.
    I thought, for example, we might build
    A poorhouse. And while we're at it, we might combine it
    With other amenities under the same roof;
    A gaol, a hall for meetings and banquets,
    With a platform for speeches, and guest rooms
    For distinguished visitors –

BRAND. But the money – ?

MAYOR. Ah! That's the problem, as always, and that
    Is what I wanted to talk to you about.
    I need your help to raise it.

BRAND. I myself am going to build.

MAYOR. What? You? Steal my plan?

BRAND. Not exactly. (*Points out of the window.*) Look. Can
    you see that?

MAYOR. What? That great ugly building?
    That's your cowshed, isn't it?

BRAND. Not that. The little ugly one.

MAYOR. What? The church?

BRAND. I shall rebuild it.

MAYOR. Rebuild the church?

BRAND. Make it great.

MAYOR. The devil you don't! That'd ruin my plan.
We'd never get the people to subscribe to both.

BRAND. That church must come down.

MAYOR. It's always been acceptable to the people,
At least in the old days.

BRAND. Possibly, but now that time is past.
It is too small.

MAYOR. Too small? Well, I've never seen it full.

BRAND. That is because there is not space enough in it
For a single soul to rise.

MAYOR. Brand, take my advice. Leave the church alone.
It's an ancient monument! You can't
Just knock it down to satisfy a whim.
It'd be shameful, horrible, barbaric –
Besides, where will you get the money?

BRAND. I will build it with my own money.
My inheritance. All I have, to the last penny,
Shall be given to this work.

MAYOR. My dear Brand, I am dumbfounded. Such munificence
Is without precedent, even in the rich cities.
I am dumbfounded. Very well,
I withdraw my project. Make your plans.
I'll see what support I can work up for you.
We shall build the church together.

BRAND. Will you give up your plan?

MAYOR. Yes. I'd be a fool not to. If I went round
Asking for contributions for my plan,
While they knew that you were paying for yours
Out of your own pocket, whom do you think
They'd support? No, I'm with you,
I'm all for your plan. I'm very taken with it.
It's quite excited me. What a lucky chance
I happened to come and visit you this evening!

BRAND. But remember. The old church must come down.

MAYOR. You know, now that I see it in the moonlight,
With all this snow on it, it does look a bit
Tumbledown.

BRAND.   What?

MAYOR.   Brand, it is too old.
I can't think why I didn't notice it before.
We mustn't let our reverence for the past,
Or our piety, warp our judgment.

BRAND.   But suppose
Our parishioners should refuse to pull it down?

MAYOR. You leave that to me.
If I don't succeed in persuading the fools to agree,
I'll pull it down with my own hands, beam by beam.
Well, I must be off. (*Takes his hat.*) I shall have to see about
Those ragamuffins I arrested this morning.

BRAND. Ragamuffins?

MAYOR. Gipsies. I discovered them just outside the village.
Dreadful people.
I tied them up and locked them in a stable.
Two or three gave me the slip, unfortunately.
The trouble is, they belong to the parish
In a kind of way. They're my responsibility. (*Laughs.*)
Yours, too. Did you ever hear folk talk
Of that penniless lad who wanted to marry your mother?
She sent him packing, of course. He went
Half out of his mind. In the end he married
A gipsy girl, and added another one
To their numbers before he died.

BRAND. A child?

MAYOR. Yes, the gipsy Gerd. So, in a sense,
The woman who brought you into the world
Brought her here too, for the girl was conceived
As a result of his love for your mother.
Well, I mustn't stay any longer. I'll be seeing you

Again soon. Goodbye, goodbye!
Remember me to your good wife! Happy Christmas!

He goes.

BRAND. Will atonement never cease?
How strangely, how wildly the threads of fate are woven!
My poor, innocent son, so you were killed
For my mother's greed. A mad, stricken girl
Born of my mother's sin, made me choose to stay.
And so you died.
For I the Lord thy God am a jealous God
And visit the sins of the fathers upon the children
Even unto the third and fourth generation. (*Turns from
    the window.*)
The God of Justice watches over us.
He demands retribution. (*Begins to pace up and down the
    room.*) Prayer! Prayer!
How easily that word slips through our lips!
Men pray to be allowed to add their weight
To Christ's burden, they stretch their hands towards
    heaven
While they stand knee-deep in the mire of doubt.

He stops, and reflects silently.

And yet – when I was afraid – when I saw my son
Fall into his last sleep, and his mother's kisses
Could not bring back the smile to his cheek,
Did I not pray then? Whence came that sweet delirium,
That stream of song, that melody
That sounded from afar, and floated by,
And bore me high and set me free? Did I pray?
Was I refreshed by prayer? Did I speak with God?
Did He hear me? Did He look down
On this house of grief where I wept? I do not know.
Now all is shut and barred. Darkness has fallen

On me again, and I can find no light,
No light. (*Cries.*) Light, Agnes! Bring me light!

AGNES *opens the door and enters with the Christmas candles. Their
bright light illumines the room.*

BRAND. Light!
AGNES. Look, Brand! The Christmas candles.
BRAND (*softly*). Ah, the Christmas candles.
AGNES (*putting them on the table*). Have I been long?
BRAND. No, no.
AGNES. How cold it is in here. You must be freezing.
BRAND. No.
AGNES (*smiles*). How proud you are.
    You will not admit that you need light and warmth.
BRAND. Hm! Will not!
AGNES (*speaks quietly as she decorates the room*).
    Last Christmas he groped
    With his tiny fingers at their clear flames.
    He stretched forward from his little chair and asked:
    'Mother, is it the sun?' (*Moves the candles slightly.*)
    They will stand here.
                          Now their light falls
    On his – on the –! Now from where he sleeps,
    He can see their warmth through the window pane.
    Now he can peep quietly in, and see
    The bright glow of our Christmas room.
    But the window pane is misted. Wait a moment.
    Wait a moment! It will soon be clear.

    She wipes the window.

BRAND. What are you doing, Agnes?
AGNES. Ssh! Quiet!
BRAND. Close the shutters.
AGNES. Brand!
BRAND. Shut them! Shut them tightly!

AGNES. Why must you be so hard? It is not right.

BRAND. Close the shutters.

AGNES (*closes them and bursts into tears*).

    How much more will you demand of me?

BRAND. Unless you give all, you give nothing.

AGNES. I have given all.

BRAND (*shakes his head*). There is more.

AGNES (*smiles*). Ask. I have the courage of poverty.

BRAND. You have your grief, your memories,

    Your sinful longing for what is gone.

AGNES. Take them, take them!

BRAND. Your sacrifice is worthless, if you grieve.

AGNES (*shudders*). Your Lord's way is steep and narrow.

BRAND. It is the way of the will. There is no other.

AGNES. But the way of mercy?

BRAND. Is built of sacrificial stones.

AGNES (*trembling*).

    Now those words of the scripture open before me

    Like a great abyss.

BRAND. Which words?

AGNES. He dies who sees Jehovah face to face.

BRAND (*throws his arms round her and holds her tightly*).

    Oh, hide, hide. Do not look at Him. Close your eyes.

AGNES. Shall I?

BRAND (*releasing her*). No.

AGNES. Brand!

BRAND. I love you.

AGNES. Your love is hard.

BRAND. Too hard?

AGNES. Do not ask. I follow where you lead.

BRAND. You are my wife, and I have the right to demand

    That you shall devote yourself wholly to our calling.

He turns to go.

AGNES. Yes. But don't leave me.

BRAND. I must. I need rest and quiet.
   Soon I shall begin to build my church. (*Embraces her.*)
   All peace be with you.

   He goes towards the door.

AGNES. Brand, may I open the shutters just a little ?
   Only a little ? Please, Brand.
BRAND (*in the doorway*). No.

   He goes into his room.

AGNES. Shut. Everything is shut.
   Even oblivion is shut to me.
   I cannot forget, and I am forbidden to weep.
   I must go out. I cannot breathe
   In this shuttered room alone. Out ? But where ?
   Will not those stern eyes in heaven follow me ?
   Can I fly from the empty silence of my fear ?

   She listens for a moment at BRAND'S *door.*

   He is reading aloud. He cannot hear what I say.
   No help, no advice, no comfort. (*Goes cautiously to the
        window.*)
   Shall I open the shutters, so that the clear light
   May hunt the horrors of night from his black bed-
        chamber ?
   No, he is not down there. Christmas
   Is the children's time. He will be allowed to come here.
   Perhaps he stands outside now, stretching up his hands
   To tap at his mother's window, and finds it closed.
   Ulf, the house is closed;
   Your father closed it. I dare not open it now.
   You and I have never disobeyed him.
   Fly back to heaven. There is light
   And happiness, there children play.
   But do not let anyone see you cry. Do not say

Your father shut you out. A little child
Cannot understand what grown people must do.
Say he was grieved, say he sighed,
Tell them it was he who plucked the pretty leaves
To make your wreath. (*Listens and shakes her head.*)
          No, I am dreaming.
There is much to be done before we two
Can meet. I must work, work silently.
God's demand must be fulfilled. I must
Make myself hard. I must make my will strong.
But tonight is Christmas, a holy night.
I will bring out my relics of love
And happiness, whose worth only a mother can know.

She kneels by a chest of drawers, opens a drawer and takes out various objects. As she does this, BRAND *opens his door and is about to speak to her when he sees what she is doing and remains silent.* AGNES *does not see him.*

AGNES. Here is the veil. Here is the shawl
    In which he was carried to his christening.
    Here is the shirt. Dear God!

She holds it up, looks at it, and smiles.

How pretty it is. How smart he looked in it
When he sat in church. Here is his scarf,
And the coat he wore when he first went out of doors.
It was too long, but it soon became too small.
Ah, and here are the clothes I wrapped him in
To keep him warm on the long journey south.
When I put them away, I was tired to death.
BRAND. Spare me, God. I cannot destroy this last idol.
    Send another, if it be Thy will.
AGNES. It is wet. Have I been crying?
    How rich I am to have these treasures still!

There is a loud knock at the door. AGNES *turns with a cry, and sees* BRAND. *The door is flung open, and a* GIPSY WOMAN *in rags rushes in with a child in her arms.*

GIPSY (*sees the child's clothes on the floor, and shouts at* AGNES).
    Share with me, rich mother.
AGNES. You are far richer than I.
GIPSY. Oh, you're like the rest. Full of words.
BRAND (*goes towards her*). Tell me what you want.
GIPSY. Not you, you're the priest. I'd rather go back
  Into the storm than have you preach at me.
  Can I help being what I am?
AGNES. Rest, and warm yourself by the fire.
  If your child is hungry, it will be fed.
GIPSY. Gipsies mustn't stay where there's light and warmth.
  We must wander, we must be on the road.
  Houses and homes are for you others.
  Just give me a rag to wrap him in. Look at him,
  He's half naked and blue with cold.
  The wind's made his body raw.
BRAND. Agnes.
AGNES. Yes?
BRAND. You see your duty.
AGNES. Brand! To her? No!
GIPSY. Give them to me. Give them all to me.
  Rags or silks, nothing's too poor or too fine
  As long as it's something to wrap him in
  And keep him warm.
BRAND. Choose, Agnes.
GIPSY. Give them to me.
AGNES. It is sacrilege. A sin against the dead.
BRAND. If you fail now, he will have died for nothing.
AGNES. Come, woman, take them. I will share them with you.
BRAND. Share, Agnes? Share?
AGNES. Half is enough. She needs no more.

BRAND. Would half have been enough for your child?
AGNES. Come, woman. Take them. Take the dress
   He wore to his baptism. Here is his shirt, his scarf,
   His coat. It will keep the night air from your child.
GIPSY. Give them to me.
BRAND. Agnes, have you given her all?
AGNES. Here is his christening robe. Take that, too.
GIPSY. Good. That seems to be all. I'll go.
   I'll wrap him up outside. Then I'll be on my way. (*Goes.*)
AGNES. Tell me, Brand. Haven't I given enough now?
BRAND. Did you give them willingly?
AGNES. No.
BRAND. Then your gift is nothing. The demand remains.

He turns to go.

AGNES (*is silent until he is almost at the door, then cries*). Brand!
BRAND. What is it?
AGNES. I lied. (*Shows him a child's cap.*)
   Look. I kept one thing.
BRAND. The cap?
AGNES. Yes.
BRAND. Stay with your idols. (*Turns.*)
AGNES. Wait!
BRAND. What do you want?
AGNES (*holds out the cap to him*). Oh, you know.
BRAND (*turns*). Willingly?
AGNES. Willingly.
BRAND. Give it to me. The woman is still outside. (*Goes.*)

AGNES *stands motionless for a moment. Gradually the expression
on her face changes to one of exultation.* BRAND *comes back. She
runs joyfully towards him, and throws her arms round his neck.*

AGNES. I am free, Brand! I am free!
BRAND. Agnes!

AGNES. The darkness is past. The mist has stolen away.
     The clouds have gone. Through the night, beyond death,
     I see the morning.
BRAND. Agnes! Yes; you have conquered.
AGNES. Yes, I have conquered now. Conquered death
     And fear. He was born to die. Ulf is in heaven.
     If I dared, if I could, I would not beg for him back again.
     Giving my child has saved my soul from death.
     Thank you for guiding my hand. You have fought for me
     Unflinchingly. Now the weight has fallen on you –
     Of All or Nothing. Now you stand
     In the valley of choice.
BRAND. Agnes, you speak in riddles. Our struggle is over.
AGNES. Have you forgotten, Brand?
     He dies who sees Jehovah face to face.
BRAND. No! Agnes, no! You shall not leave me.
     Let me lose everything else, everything,
     But not you. Don't leave me, Agnes!
AGNES. Choose. You stand where the road divides.
     Quench the light that burns in me. Give me back
     My idols. The woman is still outside.
     Let me go back to my blindness. Push me back
     Into the mire where till now I have sinned.
     You can do anything. You are free to.
     I have no strength to oppose you. If you will,
     And dare do it, I am your wife as before.
     Choose.
BRAND. Agnes, you must not go back.
     Oh, far from this place, far from our memories of sorrow,
     You will find that life and light are one.
AGNES. Do you forget the thousand souls here
     Whom God has called you to save? Whom your God bade
          you lead
     Home to the fountain of redemption? Choose.
BRAND. I have no choice.

AGNES (*embraces him*).

> Thank you for this. Thank you for everything.
>
> I am tired now. I must sleep.

BRAND. Sleep, Agnes. Your day's work is ended.

AGNES. The day is ended, and the candle is lit for the night.

> The victory took all my strength.
>
> O, but God is easy to praise! Goodnight, Brand.

BRAND. Goodnight.

AGNES. Goodnight. Thank you for everything.

> Now I want to sleep. (*Goes.*)

BRAND. Soul, be steadfast to the end.

> The victory of victories is to lose everything.
>
> Only that which is lost remains eternal.

Act Five

Six months later. The new church is ready, and stands decorated for the ceremony of consecration. The river runs close by. It is early morning, and misty. The SEXTON *is hanging garlands outside the church. After a few moments, the* SCHOOLMASTER *enters.*

SCHOOLMASTER. Good morning! My word!
    The village has come to life today.
    People are pouring in from miles around.
    The whole fjord's white with sails.
SEXTON. Yes. The people have woken up.
    It's not like the old days. Then we slept.
    Life used to be peaceful. Now they have
    To change everything. Well, I don't know.
SCHOOLMASTER. Life, sexton, life.
SEXTON. What has life to do with us?
SCHOOLMASTER. Ah, we are not ordinary parishioners.
    We are public officials. Our task
    Is to keep church discipline and instruct the young,
    And stand aloof from all controversy.
SEXTON. The priest's the cause of it all.
SCHOOLMASTER. He's no right to be. But he's no fool. He
      knows
    What impresses people. So he builds his church.
    As soon as people see something being done,
    They go crazy. It doesn't matter what it is,
    As long as something's being done.
SEXTON. Ssh!
SCHOOLMASTER. What is it?
SEXTON. Quiet!
SCHOOLMASTER. Good gracious, someone's playing the organ.

SEXTON. It's him.

SCHOOLMASTER. Who? The priest?

SEXTON. Exactly.

SCHOOLMASTER. He's out early. He doesn't sleep well these
        days.

SEXTON. He's been gnawed by loneliness ever since he lost his
        wife.

He tries to keep his sorrow to himself,

But it breaks out now and then. Listen!

Every note sounds as though he were weeping

For his wife and child.

SCHOOLMASTER. It's as if they were talking.

SEXTON. As if one were weeping, the other consoling.

The new church hasn't brought him much happiness.

SCHOOLMASTER. Or any of us. The day the old church fell

It seemed to take with it everything

In which our life had been rooted.

SEXTON. They shouted: 'Down with it, down with it!'

But when the beams began to fall,

They dropped their eyes guiltily, as though a sacrilege

Had been committed against the old house of God.

SCHOOLMASTER. As long as the new church was unfinished

They still felt they belonged to the old.

But, as the spire climbed upwards, they grew uneasy.

And now, yes, now the day has come.

How quiet everything is. They are afraid,

As though they had been summoned to elect

A new God. Where is the priest?

I feel frightened.

SEXTON. So do I, so do I!

SCHOOLMASTER. We must not forget ourselves. We are men,

Not children. Good morning. My pupils are waiting.

He goes.

SEXTON. I must get to work. Idleness is the Devil's friend.

He goes.

The organ, which has been subdued during the preceding dialogue, peals once loudly, ending in a harsh discord. A few moments later, BRAND *comes out of the church.*

BRAND. No. I can find no harmony. Only discord.
    The walls and roof imprison the music,
    As a coffin imprisons a corpse.
    I have tried, I have tried; the organ has lost its tongue.
    I lifted its voice in prayer, but it was thrown back
    Broken, like the note of a cracked and rusted bell.
    It was as if the Lord God stood enthroned
    On high in the choir, and cast it down in His wrath,
    Refusing my petition.
    'I shall rebuild the Lord's house and make it greater' –
    That was my boast. Is this what I envisaged?
    Is this the vision I once had
    Of a vault spanning the world's pain?
    If Agnes had lived, it would have been different.
    She would have banished my doubts.
    She could see greatness where I saw only smallness.

He sees the decorations.

    Garlands. Flags. They have set up my name in gold.
    God, give me light, or else bury me
    A thousand fathoms in the earth.
    Everyone praises me, but their words burn me.
    If I could hide myself. If only I could hide.
MAYOR (*enters in full uniform, and hails* BRAND *triumphantly*).
    Well, the great day's arrived! Warmest congratulations,
    My noble friend! You are a mighty man.
    Your name will soon be famous throughout the land.
    Congratulations! I feel moved, deeply moved,
    But very happy. And you?
BRAND. As though a hand were pressed around my throat.

MAYOR. Well, we mustn't have that. You must preach your
        best
    This morning. The new church has marvellous acoustics.
    Everyone I've spoken to is full of admiration.
BRAND. Really?
MAYOR. Yes. The provost himself was quite amazed,
    And praised them highly. What a noble building
    It is! What style! What size!
BRAND. You think that?
MAYOR. Think what?
BRAND. That it seems big?
MAYOR. Seems? Why, it is big.
BRAND. Yes, so it is.
    We have only exchanged an old lie for a new.
    They used to say: 'How old our church is!' Now
    They squeal: 'How big! How wonderfully big!'
    They must be told the truth. The church, as it stands,
    Is small. To hide that would be to lie.
MAYOR. God bless my soul, what strange words! What do you
        mean?
    But I've news for you. That's why I came.
    Your fame has spread, and now you have attracted
    Favourable attention in the highest circles.
    Royalty! You're to receive a decoration!
    It will be presented to you this morning.
    The Grand Cross.
BRAND. I am already crushed beneath a heavier cross.
    Let who can take that from me.
MAYOR. What? You don't seem very excited by the news.
BRAND. Oh, it's useless.
    You don't understand a word I say.
    I'm tired. Go and chatter to someone else.

He turns and walks towards the church.

MAYOR. Well, really! He must have been drinking. (*Goes.*)

BRAND. Oh, Agnes, Agnes, why did you fail me?
     I am weary of this game which no one wins
     And no one loses. I am tired of fighting alone.

Enter PROVOST.

PROVOST. Dear children! Blessed lambs! I beg your pardon –
     My sermon! I've been practising it all morning.
     Thank you, dear brother, thank you.
     My heartfelt thanks. Others more eloquent
     And wittier than I will thank you at greater length
     After luncheon. There will be many speeches.
     But, my dear Brand, you look so pale.
BRAND. My strength and courage failed me long ago.
PROVOST. Quite understandable.
     So many things to worry about, and no one
     To help you. But now the worst is over.
     Your fellow-priests are deeply proud of you,
     And the humble people are full of gratitude.
     Heartfelt gratitude. Everyone says the same
     About the church. 'What style! What size!'
     And the luncheon! My goodness, what a banquet!
     I was there just now, and watched them roasting the ox.
     You never saw a finer animal.
     They must have gone to a lot of trouble
     With meat as expensive as it is these days.
     But we mustn't ask about that. There was something else
     I wanted to talk to you about.
BRAND. Speak.
PROVOST. Well, now, you mustn't think I'm angry with you.
     You're young, you're new. You're from the city,
     And don't know country people's ways.
     To speak plainly, my complaint is this.
     You treat each one of your parishioners
     As though he were a separate spiritual problem.
     Between ourselves, that's a mistake.

You must treat all alike. We can't afford to discriminate.

BRAND. Explain yourself more clearly.

PROVOST. What I mean is this.

The state sees religion as the best means
Of improving the country's moral tone.
The best insurance against unrest.
Good Christian means good citizen.
Now the state can only achieve this
Through its officials; in this case, the priests.

BRAND. Go on.

PROVOST. Your church is of benefit to the state, and therefore
You have a responsibility to the state.
With the gift goes an obligation.

BRAND. By God, I never meant that.

PROVOST. Well, now, my friend, it's too late.

BRAND. Too late? We shall see about that.

PROVOST. I don't want to argue. I'm not asking you to do
Anything wicked. I really can't see what worries you.
You can minister just as well to the souls in your care
By serving the state at the same time.
Your job isn't to save every Jack and Jill
From damnation, but to see that the parish as a whole
Finds grace. We want all men to be equal.
But you are creating inequality
Where it never existed before. Until now
Each man was a member of the Church.
You have taught him to look upon himself
As an individual, requiring special treatment.
This will result in the most frightful confusion.
The surest way to destroy a man
Is to turn him into an individual.
Very few men can fight the world alone.

BRAND. Do you know what you are asking me to do?
You are demanding that, at the cock-crow of the state,
I shall betray the ideal for which I have lived.

PROVOST. Betray an ideal? My dear Brand, nobody
          Is asking you to do anything of the sort.
          I'm just showing you your duty.
          I only ask you to subdue those talents
          Which are not useful to our community.
          Aspire to be a saint, but be a good fellow
          And keep such aspirations to yourself.
          Don't encourage others to imitate you.
          Why be obstinate? You'll suffer for it in the end.
BRAND. I can see the mark of Cain upon your brow.
       Cowardice, greed and worldly wisdom
       Have slain the pure Abel that once dwelt in you.
PROVOST. There's no call to get personal. I don't intend
          To prolong this argument. I merely beg you
          To consider your position if you want to get on.
          Every man must curb his individuality,
          Humble himself, and not always be trying
          To rise above his fellows. The man who fights alone
          Will never achieve anything of lasting value.
          Well, goodbye. I am going to preach a sermon
          On the duality of human nature,
          And must take a little light refreshment first. (*Goes.*)
BRAND. No. Not yet. They have not got me yet.
       This churchyard has had blood to drink.
       My light, my life, lie buried here,
       But they will not get my soul.
       It is terrible to stand alone.
       Wherever I look, I see death.
       It is terrible to hunger for bread
       When every hand offers me a stone.
       If only one person would share my faith,
       And give me strength, give me peace.

EJNAR, *pale and emaciated and dressed in black, comes down the
road. He stops on seeing* BRAND.

BRAND. Ejnar! You!

EJNAR. Yes, that is my name.

BRAND. I have been longing to meet someone whose heart
  Was not of wood or stone. Come and talk to me.

EJNAR. I need no priest. I have found peace.

BRAND. You are angry with me for what happened
  When we last met.

EJNAR.   No, I do not blame you.
  You are the blind guide Our Saviour sent me
  When I was playing the world's wild game,
  Wandering in the vacant paths of sin.

BRAND. What language is this?

EJNAR.   The language of peace.
  The language a man learns when he shakes off
  The sleep of sin and wakes regenerated.

BRAND. Strange. I had heard –

EJNAR. I was seduced by pride, and belief
  In my own strength. But, God be praised,
  He did not abandon his foolish sheep.
  When the moment was ripe, He opened my eyes.

BRAND. How?

EJNAR. I fell.

BRAND. Fell?

EJNAR. Yes, into drunkenness and gambling.
  He gave me a taste for cards and dice –

BRAND. And you call this the Lord's doing?

EJNAR. That was my first step towards salvation.
  Then He took my health from me, my talent
  For painting, and my love of merriment.
  I was taken to hospital, where I lay sick
  A long while, lay as though in flames.
  I thought I saw in all the rooms
  Thousands of huge flies. At last they let me go,
  And I became a child of the Lord.

BRAND. And then?

EJNAR. I became a preacher of total abstinence,
    And am now a missionary.
BRAND. A missionary? Where?
EJNAR. In Africa. I am on my way there now.
    I must go. My time is short.
BRAND. Won't you stay for a while? As you see,
    We have a feast-day here.
EJNAR.   Thank you, no.
    My place is with the black souls. Goodbye.
BRAND. Don't you want to ask what happened to – ?
EJNAR. To whom? Ah, that young woman
    Who held me struggling in her net of lust,
    Before I became cleansed by the True Faith.
    Yes, what's happened to her?
BRAND. The next year, she became my wife.
EJNAR. Such matters do not concern me.
BRAND. Our life together was richly blessed
    With joy, and sorrow. Our child died –
EJNAR. A triviality.
BRAND. Perhaps you are right. He was lent, not given.
    And we shall meet again. But then
    She left me, too. Their graves grow green
    Side by side.
EJNAR. Vanity, Brand, vanity.
BRAND. That too?
EJNAR. All that is important is how she died.
BRAND. In hope of the dawn, with the heart's wealth untouched,
    Her will steadfast even to her last night,
    Grateful for all that life had given her
    And had taken away, she went to her grave.
EJNAR. Vanity, vanity, man. How was her faith?
BRAND. Unshakable.
EJNAR. In whom?
BRAND. In her God.
EJNAR. Her God cannot save her. She is damned.

BRAND. What are you saying?

EJNAR. Damned, poor soul.

BRAND (*calmly*). Go your way, fool.

EJNAR. The prince of darkness will have you in his clutches.
You will burn, like her, in everlasting fire.

BRAND. You dare to pronounce judgment on her and me,
Poor, sinning fool?

EJNAR. My faith has washed me clean.

BRAND. Hold your tongue.

EJNAR. Hold yours. I smell sulphur here,
And glimpse the Devil's horns upon your brow.
I am a grain of God's immortal wheat,
But you are chaff upon the wind of Judgment.

He goes.

BRAND (*stares after him for a moment, then his eyes flame and he
cries*).
And that was the man who was to give me strength!
Now all my bonds are broken. I shall march
Under my own flag, even if none will follow.

MAYOR (*enters in haste*).
Hurry, Brand! The procession is lined up
Ready to move towards the church.

BRAND. Let them come.

MAYOR. Without you? Listen, the crowd is shouting for you.
Go and calm them, or I fear they'll grow violent.

BRAND. I shall stay here.

MAYOR. Are you mad? Use your influence to control them.
Ah, it's too late.

*The crowd streams in, forcing its way through the decorations
towards the church.*

CROWD. Father! Brand! Where is the priest?
Look! There he is! Open the church, father! Open the
church!

PROVOST (*to* MAYOR). Cannot you control them?

MAYOR. They won't pay any attention to me.

BRAND. At last a current has stirred this stagnant pool.

    Men, you stand at the crossroads! Will yourselves to be
       new!

    Destroy everything in you that is rotten!

    Only then can the great temple be built,

    As it must and shall.

PRIESTS AND OFFICIALS. The priest is mad. He is mad.

BRAND. Yes, I was. I was mad to think

    That to double the church's size would be enough.

    I did not see that it was All or Nothing.

    I lost myself in compromise. But today

    The Lord has spoken. The trump of doom

    Has sounded over this house. Now all doubt is past.

    People! Compromise is the way of Satan!

CROWD (*in fury*). Away with them, they have blinded us.

    Away with them, they have stolen our spirit.

BRAND. No. Your enemy lurks within you, binding you;

    A worm sapping your strength.

    Why have you come to the church? Only

    To gape at the show, to gape at its steeple,

    To listen to the organ and the bells,

    Enjoy the glow of high-sounding speeches.

    This was not what I dreamed.

    I dreamed that I might build a church so great

    That it would embrace, not just faith and doctrine,

    But everything in life

    Which God has given as a part of life.

    The day's toil, the evening's rest, the night's

    Sorrows, the fresh delights of burning youth,

    The river that flows below, the waterfall

    That roars between the rocks, the cry of the storm,

    And the soft voices that call from the sea.

    These should be one with the Word of God,

    With the organ music and the people's singing.

The thing that stands here is a lie, a monstrous lie!
Away with it!

CROWD. Lead us! Lead us! Lead us to victory!

PROVOST. Do not listen to him. He is not a true Christian.

BRAND. No, you are right. I am not a true Christian.
Neither are you, nor is anyone here.
A true Christian must have a soul,
And show me one who has kept his soul!
You grind away God's image, live like beasts,
Then join the grovelling queue to beg for grace.
Has He not said that only if ye are
As little children can ye enter the kingdom?
Come then, both men and women;
Show yourselves with fresh children's faces
In the great church of life!

MAYOR. Open the door!

CROWD (*cries as though in anguish*).
No, not this church! Not this church! The church of life!

BRAND. Our church is boundless. It has no walls.
Its floor is the green earth,
The moorland, the meadow, the sea, the fjord.
Only heaven can span its roof.
There, life and faith shall melt together.
The day's toil there is a flight among the stars,
Is one with children's play round the Christmas tree,
Is one with the dance of the king before the ark.

*A storm seems to shake the crowd. Some turn away, but most of
them press closer round* BRAND.

CROWD. You give us light! We have lived in darkness!
Show us the Church of Life! Life and faith must be one!

PROVOST. Stop him, stop him! He will take our flock from us.

MAYOR (*quietly*). Keep calm, man. Let him rave.

BRAND (*to* CROWD). Away from this place! God is not here.
His kingdom is perfect freedom.

He locks the church door, and stands with the keys in his hand.

I am priest here no longer. I withdraw my gift.

He throws the keys into the river.

If you want to enter, creep in through the cellars.
Your backs are supple.

MAYOR (*quietly, relieved*).
Well, that's the end of his decoration.

PROVOST. He'll never be a bishop now.

BRAND. Come, all you who are young and strong!
Leave this dead valley! Follow me to victory!
One day you must awaken! Arise
From your misery! Arise from your half-life!
Slay the enemy within you!

MAYOR. Stop! Stop!

CROWD. Show us the way! We will follow!

BRAND. Over the frozen ocean of the moor!
We shall wander through the land, freeing
Our souls, purifying, crushing our weakness.
Be men, be priests, renew God's faded image.
Make the earth your temple.

The CROWD, *including the* SCHOOLMASTER *and the* SEXTON, *swarm around him. They raise* BRAND *high on their shoulders.*

CROWD. A vision! Follow him! Arise!
Leave the valley! Up to the moor!

They stream up through the valley. A few remain behind.

PROVOST. Are you blind? Can't you see that the devil is in his
words?

MAYOR. Turn back, turn back!
You belong to the calm waters of this village.
Good people, stop! He will lead you to destruction.
Listen! They will not answer, the swine!

PROVOST. Think of your homes and houses.

CROWD. A greater house shall be built.

MAYOR. How will you live?

CROWD. The chosen people found manna in the wilderness.

PROVOST (*gazes after them with folded hands, and says quietly*).

   They have left me. My flock has abandoned me.

MAYOR. Do not fear, my lord. Victory will soon be ours.

PROVOST (*almost in tears*).

   Victory? But our flock has left us.

MAYOR. We are not beaten. Not if I know my sheep.

He goes after them. The PROVOST *follows.*

*By the highest farm above the village. A bleak mountain landscape
towers behind. It is raining.* BRAND *appears over the hillside,
followed by the crowd of men, women and children.*

BRAND. Forward! Forward! Victory lies ahead.

   Forget your village. Leave it in its hollow.

   The mist has buried it. Forget that you were beasts.

   Now you are men of the Lord. Climb onward, climb!

A MAN. Wait, wait. My old father is tired.

ANOTHER. I have eaten nothing since yesterday.

SEVERAL. Yes, give us food. Quench our thirst.

BRAND. We must cross the mountain first. Follow me.

MAN. The path's too steep. We'll never get there by nightfall.

SEXTON. The Ice Church lies that way.

BRAND. The steep path is the shortest.

A WOMAN. My child is sick.

ANOTHER WOMAN. My feet are sore.

A THIRD. Water, water, we are thirsty.

SCHOOLMASTER. Give them strength, priest. Their courage
         is failing.

CROWD. Perform a miracle, father. A miracle.

BRAND. Your slavery has branded you vilely.

   You demand your wage before your work is done.

Rise up, shake off your sloth.

If you cannot, go back to your graves.

SCHOOLMASTER. He is right, victory must be won first.

The reward will follow.

BRAND. You will be rewarded, my people,

As surely as a God watches keen-eyed over this world.

CROWD. He prophesies! He prophesies!

OTHERS IN THE CROWD. Tell us, priest, will the battle be
hard?

Will it be long? Will it be bloody?

A MAN. Will we have to be brave?

SCHOOLMASTER. There's no question of our lives being
endangered?

A MAN. What will be my share of the reward?

A WOMAN. My son will not die, will he, father?

SEXTON. Will victory be ours by Tuesday?

BRAND (*stares at them bewildered*).

What are you asking? What do you want to know?

SEXTON. First, how long shall we have to fight?

Secondly, how much will it cost us?

Thirdly, what will be our reward?

BRAND. That is what you want to know?

SCHOOLMASTER. Yes; you didn't tell us.

BRAND (*angrily*). Then I shall tell you now.

CROWD. Speak! Speak!

BRAND. How long will you have to fight? Until you die!

What will it cost? Everything you hold dear.

Your reward? A new will, cleansed and strong,

A new faith, integrity of spirit;

A crown of thorns. That will be your reward.

CROWD (*screams in fury*). Betrayed! You have betrayed us!

You have tricked us!

BRAND. I have not betrayed or tricked you.

CROWD. You promised us victory. Now you ask for sacrifice.

BRAND. I have promised you victory,

And I swear it shall be won through you.

But we who march in the first rank must fall.

CROWD. He wants us to die! To save people who haven't been
born!

BRAND. The only road to Canaan lies through a desert.

That desert is self-sacrifice. Death is the only victory.

I consecrate you soldiers of the Lord.

SCHOOLMASTER. We can't go back.

SEXTON. And we daren't go on.

WOMEN (*pointing in terror down the road*).

Look! The provost!

SCHOOLMASTER. Now don't be frightened.

Enter PROVOST.

PROVOST. My children! My sheep! Listen to the voice

Of your old shepherd. Do not listen

To this man. He would trick you with false promises.

CROWD. That's true.

PROVOST. We understand weakness. We forgive those

Who truly repent. Look into your hearts

Before it is too late.

Can you not see the black art he has used

To get you into his power?

CROWD. Yes. He has bewitched us.

PROVOST. Think, my children. What can you achieve,

Humble people born in a humble village?

Were you created to shake the world,

To right wrongs, liberate the oppressed?

You have your humble tasks allotted you;

To attempt more is presumptuous and wrong.

Would you intervene between the hawk and the eagle?

Would you challenge the wolf and the bear?

You will only be preyed on by the ruthless and the mighty,

My sheep, my children.

CROWD. Yes. It's true. He's right.

BRAND. Choose, men and women. Choose.
SOME OF THE CROWD. We want to go home.
OTHERS. Too late, too late. Let us go on.
MAYOR (*hurries in*). What luck that I managed to find you!
WOMEN. Oh, sir, please don't be angry with us.
MAYOR. No time for that. Just you come with me.
     A marvellous thing has happened for the village.
     If you behave sensibly, you will all be rich by nightfall.
CROWD. What? How?
MAYOR. A shoal of fishes has entered the fjord –
     Millions of them!
CROWD. What?
MAYOR. Do you want to spend the night on this mountain?
     Such a shoal has never entered our fjord before.
     A better time is dawning for us, my friends.
BRAND. Choose between him and God.
PROVOST. A miracle! A miracle! A sign from Heaven!
     I have often dreamed that this might happen.
     Now it has. We have been given a sign.
BRAND. If you turn back now, you are lost.
CROWD. A shoal of fishes!
MAYOR. Millions of them!
PROVOST. Food for your children! Gold for your wives!
SEXTON. Will I be allowed to keep my job?
SCHOOLMASTER. Will my school be taken from me?
PROVOST. Use your good influence with the people, and you
          will find us lenient.
MAYOR. Away, away! Don't waste time!
SEXTON. To the boats, to the boats!
SOME OF THE CROWD. What about the priest?
SCHOOLMASTER. The priest? Leave the lunatic.
CROWD. Yes – he lied to us!
PROVOST. He refused his old mother the sacrament.
MAYOR. He killed his child.
SEXTON. And his wife too.

WOMEN. Shame on him! The scoundrel!

PROVOST. A bad son, a bad father, a bad husband.
Where could you find a worse Christian?

CROWD. He pulled our church down. He locked us out of the
new one.

BRAND. I see the mark of Cain on every brow.
I see where you will all end.

CROWD (*roars*). Don't listen to him!
Drive the hell-brand away from the village!
Stone him! Kill him!

They stone BRAND *and drive him up the mountain. Gradually
his pursuers return.*

PROVOST. Oh, my children! Oh, my sheep!
Return to your firesides. Repent of your rash folly,
And you will find that the simple life is good.
Farewell – and good luck to your fishing!

SEXTON. They are true Christians. They are gentle and
merciful.

SCHOOLMASTER. They go their way and let us go ours.

SEXTON. They don't ask us to sacrifice our lives.

SCHOOLMASTER. They are wise.

The CROWD *goes down towards the village.*

PROVOST. God's miracle has saved us.

MAYOR. What miracle?

PROVOST. The shoal of fishes.

MAYOR. Oh, that. A lie, of course.

PROVOST. A lie? Really? Well, I –

MAYOR. I hope your reverence will think it excusable,
In view of the importance of the issue.

PROVOST. Of course, of course. Quite excusable.

MAYOR (*scratches his nose*).
I wonder, though, whether their treatment of him
Wasn't a little inhumane?

PROVOST. The voice of the people is the voice of God.
  Come!
  They go.

Among the peaks. A storm is gathering, hunting the clouds slowly across the snowfields. Black peaks are visible here and there; then they are veiled again in mist. BRAND *appears, blood-stained and beaten.*

BRAND (*stops and looks back*). A thousand started with me
      from the valley;
  Not one has followed me to the mountain top.
  All of them have the craving in their hearts,
  But the sacrifice frightens them.
  Their will is weak; their fear is strong.
  Someone once died to save their souls,
  So nothing more is required of them.

He sinks down on a stone.

  It was not for us that He drained the cup of agony,
  Not for us that the thorn-crown scarred His brow.
  It was not for us that the lance pierced His side,
  Not for us that the nails burned
  Through His hands and feet. We are small and mean.
  We are not worthy. We defy the call to arms.
  It was not for us that He carried His cross.

He throws himself down into the snow and covers his face. After a while he looks up.

  Have I been dreaming? Am I awake?
  Everything is hidden in mist. Was it all
  Only a sick man's vision? Have we forgotten
  The image in whose likeness we were made?
  Is Man defeated after all? (*Listens.*)
  Ah! There is a sound in the air like singing.

VOICES (*murmur in the storm*).

> You can never be like Him, for you are flesh.
>
> Do His will, or forsake Him, you are lost, lost.

BRAND. Lost. Lost? I can almost believe it.

> Did He not reject my prayer in the church?
>
> Did He not take from me all I had,
>
> Closed every path that might have led me to light?
>
> Made me fight until my strength was finished,
>
> And then let me be defeated?

VOICES (*louder*). Worm, you will never be like Him.

> You have drained the cup of death.
>
> Follow or forsake Him, your work is doomed.

BRAND (*weeps quietly*). Ulf and Agnes, come back to me.

> I sit alone on the mountain top.
>
> The north wind blows through me, spectres haunt me.

He looks up. A gap opens in the mist, revealing the FIGURE OF A WOMAN, *wrapped in a light cloak. It is* AGNES.

FIGURE (*smiles, and opens her arms towards him*).

> Brand, I have come back to you.

BRAND. Agnes? Agnes! (*Moves towards her.*)

FIGURE (*screams*). Stop! A gulf lies between us.

> (*Gently.*) You are not dreaming. You are not asleep.
>
> You have been sick, my dear. You have been mad.
>
> You dreamed your wife was dead.

BRAND. You are alive? Praise be to – !

FIGURE (*quickly*). Ssh! We have not much time.

> Come with me, come with me.

BRAND. But – Ulf?

FIGURE. He is alive, too.

BRAND. Alive?

FIGURE. It was all a dream. Your sorrows were a dream.

> You fought no battle. Ulf is with your mother.
>
> She is well, and he grows tall.
>
> The old church still stands; you can pull it down, if you wish.

The villagers toil below, as they did before you came,
In the good old days.

BRAND. Good?

FIGURE. Yes. Then there was peace.

BRAND. Peace?

FIGURE. Quickly, Brand. Come with me.

BRAND. Ah, I am dreaming.

FIGURE. No longer. But you need tenderness and care.

BRAND. I am strong.

FIGURE. Not yet. Your dreams will lure you back again.
The mist will swallow you, and take you from me.
Your mind will grow confused again unless
You try the remedy.

BRAND. Oh, give it to me!

FIGURE. You have it.

BRAND. What is it?

FIGURE. Three words.
You must blot them out, wipe them from your memory.
Forget them.

BRAND. Say them!

FIGURE. All or Nothing.

BRAND (*shrinks*). Ah! That?

FIGURE. As surely as I live, and as surely as you shall sometime
die.

BRAND. Alas for us both; the drawn sword
Hangs over us as it hung before.

FIGURE. Be gentle, Brand. My breasts are warm.
Hold me in your strong arms.
Let us go and find the sun and the summer.

BRAND. The sickness will not come again.

FIGURE. It will come, Brand. Be sure.

BRAND (*shakes his head*).
No, I have put it behind me. The horror of dreams
Is past. Now comes the horror of life.

FIGURE. Of life?

BRAND. Come with me, Agnes.

FIGURE. Stop! Brand, what will you do?

BRAND. What I must. Live what till now I dreamed;
Make the illusion real.

FIGURE. Impossible! Remember where that road led you.

BRAND. I will tread it again.

FIGURE. That road of fear in the mist of dreams?
Will you ride it freely and awake?

BRAND. Freely and awake.

FIGURE. And let your child die?

BRAND. And let my child die.

FIGURE. Brand!

BRAND. I must.

FIGURE. And kill me?

BRAND. I must.

FIGURE. Quench the candles in the night,
And shut out the sun in the day?
Never pluck life's fruit, never be soothed
By song? I remember so many songs.

BRAND. I must. Do not waste your prayer.

FIGURE. Do you forget what reward your sacrifices brought
you?
Your hopes betrayed you, everyone forsook you.
Everyone stoned you.

BRAND. I do not suffer for my own reward.
I do not strive for my own victory.

FIGURE. Remember, an Angel with a flaming rod
Drove Man from Paradise.
He set a gulf before the gate.
Over that gulf you cannot leap.

BRAND. The way of longing remains.

FIGURE (*disappears; there is a clap of thunder, the mist gathers
where it stood, and a sharp and piercing scream is heard
as though from one in flight*).
Die! The world has no use for you!

BRAND (*stands for a moment as though dazed*).
    It disappeared in the mist,
    Flying on great rough wings across the moor
    Like a hawk. It was a deceitful spirit;
    The spirit of compromise.

GERD (*appears with a rifle*).
    Did you see him? Did you see the hawk?

BRAND. Yes, child. This time I saw him.

GERD. Quick, tell me – which way did he fly?
    We'll go after him. This time we'll get him.

BRAND. No weapon can harm him. You think you've killed him,
    But the next moment he's after you,
    As fierce as ever.

GERD. I stole the reindeer-hunter's rifle, and loaded it
    With silver. I'm not as mad as they say.

BRAND. I hope you hit him. (*Turns to go.*)

GERD. Priest, you're limping. Your foot's hurt.
    How did that happen?

BRAND. The people hunted me.

GERD (*goes closer*). Your forehead is red.

BRAND. The people stoned me.

GERD. Your voice used to be clear as song.
    Now it creaks like leaves in autumn.

BRAND. Everything – everyone –

GERD. What?

BRAND. Betrayed me.

GERD (*stares at him*). Ah! Now I know who you are!
    I thought you were the priest. Fie upon him and all the
        others!
    You're the Big Man. The Biggest of all.

BRAND. I used to think I was.

GERD. Let me see your hands.

BRAND. My hands?

GERD. They're scarred with nails. There's blood in your hair.
    The thorn's teeth have cut your forehead.

You've been on the cross. My father told me
It happened long ago and far away.
But now I see he was deceiving me.
I know you. You're the Saviour Man!

BRAND. Get away from me!

GERD. Shall I fall down at your feet and pray?

BRAND. Go!

GERD. You gave the blood that will save us all.
There are nail holes in your hands. You are the Chosen
One.
You are the Greatest of all.

BRAND. I am the meanest thing that crawls on earth.

GERD (*looks up; the clouds are lifting*).
Do you know where you are standing?

BRAND (*stares unseeingly*). I stand upon the lowest stair.
There is far to climb and my feet are sore.

GERD (*savagely*).
Answer me! Do you know where you are standing?

BRAND. Yes, now the mist is lifting.

GERD. Yes, it is lifting. Black Peak points its finger towards
heaven.

BRAND (*looks up*). Black Peak? The Ice Church?

GERD. Yes. You came to my church after all.

BRAND. I wish I were far away. Oh, how I long for light
And sun, and the still tenderness of peace.
I long to be where life's summer kingdoms are.
(*Weeps.*)
O Jesus, I have called upon Your name.
Why did You never receive me into Your bosom?
You passed close by me, but You never touched me.
Let me hold one poor corner of Your garment
And wet it with my tears of true repentance.

GERD (*pale*).
What's the matter? You're crying! Hot tears.
The ice in my memory is thawing into tears.

You're melting the snow on my church roof.
The ice-priest's cloak is sliding from his shoulders.
(*Trembles.*) Man, why did you never weep before?
BRAND (*serene and shining, as though young again*).
My life was a long darkness.
Now the sun is shining. It is day.
Until today I sought to be a tablet
On which God could write. Now my life
Shall flow rich and warm. The crust is breaking.
I can weep! I can kneel! I can pray! (*Sinks to his knees.*)
GERD (*looks up towards the sky and says timidly and quietly*).
Look, there he sits, the ugly brute. That's him
Casting the shadow. Can't you hear him beating
The sides of the peak with his great wings?
Now is the moment, now! If only the silver will bite!

She throws the rifle to her cheek and fires. A hollow boom, like thunder, sounds from high up on the mountain.

BRAND (*starts up*). What are you doing?
GERD. I hit him! Look, he's falling! Hear how he groans!
Look at his white feathers floating
Down the mountain side! Ah!
He's rolling down on top of us!
BRAND (*sinks exhausted*).
Must each man die to atone for human sin?
GERD. Look how he tumbles and rolls!
Oh, I shan't be afraid any more.
Why, he's as white as a dove! (*Shrieks in fear.*)
Oh, the horrid, horrid roar!
Throws herself down in the snow.

BRAND (*shrinks before the onrushing avalanche*).
Answer me, God, in the moment of death!
If not by Will, how can Man be redeemed?
The avalanche buries him, filling the whole valley.
A VOICE (*cries through the thunder*). He is the God of Love.

Note on the Translation

Ibsen composed *Brand* in rhymed octosyllabics, varying his rhyming scheme with extraordinary skill. If one listens to the play in Norwegian, one almost forgets that rhyme is being used, although it plays an important part in giving an epigrammatic point to key statements, and reinforcing the strength and dignity of the language.

The present translation avoids rhyme, but otherwise keeps closely to Ibsen's text, except where cuts have been made. Ibsen, writing in 1865, included long discussions on topical issues, such as the Schleswig-Holstein war, the need for land reform, and the danger of an industrial revolution. Although these sections still read vividly as satirical verse, they digress from the main thread of the play, and have been omitted. Other cuts have been made for the sake of dramatic concision, though these are fewer and shorter than might have been supposed necessary.

I gladly express my thanks to Michael Elliott for much patient advice; also to the 59 Theatre Company for commissioning this translation.

M.M.

Methuen Modern Plays

EDITED BY JOHN CULLEN AND GEOFFREY STRACHAN